BEARING TEARS
and
Precious Seed

The Story of Robert L. Painter

BETTY HUTCHINSON JONES

WESTBOW
PRESS®
A DIVISION OF THOMAS NELSON
& ZONDERVAN

WestBow Press books may be ordered through booksellers or by contacting:

WestBow Press
A Division of Thomas Nelson & Zondervan
1663 Liberty Drive
Bloomington, IN 47403
www.westbowpress.com
1 (866) 928-1240

ISBN: 978-1-4908-9655-7 (sc)
ISBN: 978-1-4908-9656-4 (e)

Print information available on the last page.

WestBow Press rev. date: 01/20/2016

In Memory of
Rev. Robert Lee Painter
God's missionary to the peoples of the Roanoke Valley of Virginia
&
Egyptian Villages of the Nile River

His Beloved wife,
Virginia Morgan Painter

His Beloved daughter
Gloria Painter Beckner,

For
Joyce Painter Hudson, daughter
Charlotte Painter Wimmer, daughter
&
Family and friends

Commemorating the hundredth anniversary of
Robert Lee Painter's birth

...also by Betty Hutchinson Jones

I Sense the Love of God in Seasons
Poetry-Volume I

Butterfly Wings
Poetry-Volume II

Rose from Healing Springs
Christian Novel

Bearing Tears and Precious Seed
The Robert L. Painter Story

As told by him to
Betty Hutchinson Jones

Brother Robert Lee Painter
1947

To Suffering Egyptian Christians and World Missionaries

For more than 20 years, the Egyptian people were the heartbeat of Robert Painter's foreign mission. He spent countless hours traveling up and down the Nile River to give them God's plan of salvation. No doubt, there will be an abundance of stars in his crown for those he brought to the saving knowledge of the Lord Jesus Christ. If Brother Painter were on earth today, he would tell us that when the Egyptians had so few Christians to share the gospel message with them, God honored him with the privilege. He loved the people of the Nile, and they in turn, loved him. Whenever he arrived for his annual visit, men, women and children flocked to his side, greeting him as if he were one of their own, and when the time came that he must leave, *"The Preacher"* and his converts wept together as a family. May God wrap every one of those loving Egyptian Christians in His arms, and may He open doors for them to share the Good News that they received with their families, friends and neighbors.

"He that goeth forth and weepeth, bearing precious seed,
shall doubtless come again rejoicing, bringing his sheaves with him."

Psalm 126:6

Foreword

There is always at least one individual in a lifetime who comes to us as a very special friend. In my life, that person was Brother Robert L. Painter. I thank God for the privilege of having known such a man. Challenged by his devout faith and ministry, my life was forever changed. Even today, I remain in awe of the passion he had for Christ- and for people. Brother Painter truly loved people. "John," he often said to me, "you have to love the people. Many preachers love to preach, but they do not know how to love people." Through the power of the Holy Spirit, Robert Painter lived this love. He enjoyed people of every color, size, and class, neglecting none, not even the little children.

Almost everyone called Brother Painter *"The Preacher"* and because his sermons were filled with spiritual wealth, the title was more than befitting. "Feed the people," he would say, "and they'll come back for more." I have never seen such passion as this man had for the hearts and souls of men. The entire focus of his ministry was to glorify Christ, rescue the lost and build up believers. He was a man of extraordinary gifts-gifts including those of an unusual memory and holy boldness. He preached with conviction from a heart filled with spiritual intensity, coupled with tear-filled eyes. His favorite passage of scripture comes from the book of Galatians, chapter 2, verse 20. "I am crucified with Christ: nevertheless I live; yet not I, but Christ liveth in me: and the life which I now live in the flesh I live by the faith of the Son of God, who loved me and gave himself for me."

Robert Painter was my pastor, mentor, and friend. We were blessed to travel to the land of the pyramids, and minister alongside one another in its cities, towns, and villages. Time has long since erased our footprints from the sands of Egypt, but not from the hearts of the

Egyptian people. Only eternity will reveal how the Lord used this one evangelist's extraordinary labor of love to lead so many Egyptians to Jesus Christ.

Another highlight of our travels together included visits to the Holy Land. It was a magnificent experience for Brother Painter and me to walk where Jesus walked! And how could I ever forget that morning when darkness still filled the skies, and we walked together up "Moses' Mountain"? All along the way, I could hear him humming the words from an old Negro spiritual, *"If I could, I surely would, stand on the rock where Moses stood."*

I have ministered with this man of God within the combines of our churches, standing by his side in funerals, weddings and baby dedications. We have rejoiced together, and we have wept together. I am eternally indebted to his example and discipleship. He was a gifted pastor, evangelist, missionary and friend. To most of us, however, he was simply "The Preacher". I assure you this book will introduce to you a great man, truly a monument to God's magnificent grace. I will forever love and appreciate him.

John Ingram
Pastor-Stanton Bible Methodist Church
Stanton, Alabama

Preface

I was not yet ten years old when in June of 1947 I accepted the Lord Jesus Christ as my personal Savior. Two months later, Rev. Robert L. Painter opened the doors of the House of Prayer on 17th Street in Southeast Roanoke, Virginia. I well remember the manifestations of God's Spirit and the excitement of those early years when souls found God in almost every meeting. Aside from Sunday school and regularly scheduled church meetings, Brother Painter endeavored to reach out to lost souls of our community in many ways. There were street meetings, revivals, Sunday afternoon meetings at the City Rescue Mission, outdoor meetings in Mount Pleasant, cottage prayer meetings throughout the valley, and last but not least, tremendously successful tent revivals. Children, as well as mature Christians, were encouraged to live lives separated from the world. The House of Prayer, under the leadership of Brother Painter, became a lighthouse throughout Roanoke City and the surrounding counties. Few were the nights there was not a meeting to conduct somewhere. His followers gathered in homes for cottage prayer meetings, and often huddled on street corners to sing and pray. Passersby stopped walking, residents sat on porches, and barrooms saw their customers leave the premises. All were anxious to hear the preaching of the gospel.

"The Preacher" taught his converts that they should live by the Word of God, and they, in turn, taught others. He touched the lives of many people, and many did not forget. After more than sixty years, his legacy lives on.

I met my husband, Everett Jones, through Brother Painter's 1951 tent revival in Blue Ridge, Virginia, and after our marriage, we were gone from the Roanoke area until 1995. In 1967, my mother, Dorothy

Hutchinson, learned I was going on a tour of the Middle East. She suggested that it would be an excellent gesture on the part of the House of Prayer if the church gave Brother Painter this same opportunity. His people agreed with her, and because of their decision, I had the privilege to stand at Gordon's Calvary on Easter Sunday of that year by the side of my childhood pastor.

Everyone who knew Brother Painter can testify to the profound effect that tour made on his life. While we were in Cairo, Egypt, he met a missionary who arranged for him to speak to hundreds of lost souls. That evening, while looking over the masses of this poverty-stricken land, the uneducated country preacher's heart received a burden that would not let go. For many years to come, he annually boarded a jet and became an evangelist to those Egyptian people. Up until the age of ninety, he saw thousands of people accept Jesus Christ as their personal Savior. Brother Painter answered God's call to go to the uttermost parts of the earth, and for this, the congregation of the House of Prayer must indeed be grateful. They were the dispatchers of a pastor who sacrificed much to carry out The Great Commission.

I owe much of my spiritual growth to the people of many Christian faiths. I often say the Baptists taught me the Bible, the Nazarenes led me to the Lord, and the House of Prayer led me out of worldliness. Because of his burdened heart and his desire to preach God's Word, Brother Painter is the childhood pastor I did not forget. What I remember most about him is that he lived the life he preached, and second to this, I remember the tears I saw him shed in the pulpit, tears of someone who cared for lost souls. I have always believed his life was truly a story of God's marvelous grace, and a story to share with others. When I returned to Roanoke, I told my cousin, Jean Mays Porter that if no one had ever written Brother Painter's life story, I would like to try. She was more than willing to help me contact him. Although I am a graduate of Long Ridge Writers Group and the Institute for Children's Literature, I am not a professional writer, and progress on the book has been slow. For this superlative man of God to give me the opportunity to write his story is truly an honor.

The House of Prayer is not one of America's mega-churches, and it is not "great' as men see greatness, but the magnitude of its ministries is universal. All across these United States and even around the world, Sunday school teachers, preachers, gospel singers, musicians, writers, missionaries, and others have roots planted and nourished in the confines of a little church located in the Blue Ridge Mountains of Virginia. I thank God for the ministries of the House of Prayer, and I thank Him even more for Brother Robert Painter. I am also grateful for those founders who struggled to begin this work for the Lord. I only wish they had lived long enough to see what has happened to the work they began.

Betty H. Jones-Author

Acknowledgments

Numerous individuals have contributed to the completion of this manuscript, and I am indeed grateful to everyone. Without the help of some of you, I could never have put Brother Painter's story together. Not only was his life not an ordinary life, but so much of what he accomplished happened so many years ago. Thankfully, some of you are proficient with remembering while others kept written records and photographs. Many of you were valuable to me as readers, and some encouraged me in the faith. From out of the abundance of my heart, I thank every one of you. If I have omitted any deserving person from the list, you have my apologies. The book has been in the making for many years.

Joyce Painter Hudson - Contacts, information, photographs, manuscript critique

Charlotte Painter Wimmer - Manuscript critique and information

Jean Mays Porter - Travel escort and House of Prayer history

Betty Mays Wiseman - Travel escort and House of Prayer history

Mildred Hutchinson St. Clair – Photographs, House of Prayer history, testimonial

Hillary and Betty Leonard - Testimony of Suzette's healing

Rev. Jeff Keaton - Introduction

Rev. John Ingram – Foreward

Everett L. Jones - Filming and recording of interviews, manuscript critique

Candy Jones Daniels -Typing, CDs, and Manuscript critique

Iris Thurman Robtison - House of Prayer history

Barbara Wegner - Manuscript critique

Rev. Marvin Wegner - Manuscript critique

Roger Moretz - Manuscript critique

Floyd House of Prayer - History and comments

Rev. Robert Miller - Testimonial

Debbie Eller – Manuscript critique

Rev. Aubrey Dooley - Manuscript critique

Rev. John Dooley - Manuscript critique

Joyce McPherson- Manuscript critique

Introduction

Throughout my childhood and early adult years, I heard about Robert Painter, and I knew that there was something unique and special about him. Not until I became pastor of the House of Prayer in the year 2000, did I know just how influential his ministries had been on the hearts of people in Southwest Virginia and other parts of the world. Only in eternity will we know the true impact of this one life on earth.

"Preacher Painter" founded the House of Prayer in Roanoke, Virginia in 1947 and faithfully pastored it until 1992 when he was 78 years old. Eight years later, I became its third pastor. Immediately, upon my arrival at the church, I began to hear stories about Preacher Painter. Every person who spoke of him seemed to revere him in one way or another. In the early to middle years of his pastorate, scores of people found salvation through his ministries. Many of these converts left the House of Prayer and became Christian leaders in different denominations. I have met Pentecostal pastors, Baptist pastors and Wesleyan Methodist pastors who all testify to finding salvation under Robert Painter's ministry.

If ever there was an evangelist, Preacher Painter was an evangelist. Because of his own radical conversion to Christ, he believed that Jesus could and would save anyone and everyone. He was fearless, tough and willing to work day and night in order to advance the Kingdom of Christ. He carried the gospel message to regions outside of Roanoke City, even outside of the United States. For many years, he made annual missionary trips to the land of Egypt to share the gospel with her people. If we could number his converts there, the total would probably reach into the thousands.

Shortly after becoming the pastor of the House of Prayer, I asked if the church had shown honor to Preacher Painter for his many years of service. The church board spoke of how they wanted to honor him but had never been able to do so. I quickly drove south of Roanoke to his home on top of a mountain. Even in his upper 80's, I found him just coming in out of the garden. After introducing myself, (he already knew everything about me), I asked him if he would allow us to set aside one entire Sunday to honor his ministry. Without hesitation, he smiled and said, "That will be fine."

We planned the big day, and as hundreds of people who had been touched by Preacher Painter's ministry filed in that Sunday, we had to move our service to the gymnasium. Numerous individuals gave testimonies that God used "The Preacher" to bring change in their lives. In all of my years as a pastor, that day still stands out as one of the greatest days of my ministry. I saw the day become not only one of recognition but also a day of reunion and glorious celebration. The Bible says to give honor to whom honor is due and our entire church, along with many others, was happy to honor this great man of God.

Throughout the years before his death, I had other privileges to interact with Preacher Painter. When the House of Prayer dedicated the new tabernacle at the Blue Ridge Holiness Camp in Floyd, Virginia, we named it the Painter Tabernacle. He and many of his family members were able to be with us for this grand occasion. Brother Painter was one of the founders of this camp and had invested a lifetime into the grounds and the camp's development.

The Preacher spent his closing days at his mountaintop home until his family was unable to care for him there. He then resided in a Botetourt County nursing facility. As his health began to fail and his eyesight faded, he was still as passionate about Christ as he had ever been. I often found him listening to the Bible on a CD recording, and when he had listened to it all the way through, he listened again, and then again. At the nursing home, I noticed that all of his nurses seemed to be enamored with him because, as I soon learned, he had become like a spiritual father to the staff. His nurses were asking for his prayers, and he in turn, was inviting them to accept Jesus.

Even though Preacher Painter had very little education, his passion for Christ and his love for people enabled him to influence their lives in a special way. He never strayed far from the most important issues in life. His relationship with Jesus Christ was always front and center, and he worked every day after his conversion to introduce his Savior to others. He truly believed that Jesus was the answer to all of man's problems, and as a direct or indirect result of his life, he will see untold thousands of redeemed souls in heaven.

Read Robert Painter's story and know that if God can use one humble mountain boy like him, He can also use your life to bring honor and glory to His Son!

Rev. Jeff Keaton
RENEWANATION, Founder and CEO

Chapter 01

My Humble Roots

Dec. 1913-Sept. 1928

. . . .

"Be it ever so humble, there's no place like home"

The Painters' Homestead

Hidden deep within the heart of the Blue Ridge Mountains in Rockbridge County, Virginia, the homestead where I was born on December 17, 1913, was known to all who lived there as Montebello. This area, however, was nothing more than mountains of towering timber owned by the South River Lumber Company. There, in a land of steep rugged terrain and lush green valleys, my parents, Robert Newton and Lillie Mae Grove Painter, struggled to maintain a meager existence for themselves, their seven sons, and one daughter. When an infant niece came to us in need of a home, my parents claimed her as their second daughter. We loved and cared for her as if she had been born into our family.

The aged, frame and company-owned house where we lived, was the only home my mom and dad ever shared together. My pa often said that he lived there for so long that he ought to be able to claim it. To my knowledge, he never filed such a claim. Located on a narrow piece of land between Irish Creek and a graveled state road, a range of mountains surrounded it on either side. It had no bath and no running water. Every day, we walked across the road, filled our water buckets with fresh mountain spring water, and then hauled them back home. Inside the house with creaking wooden floors, there were two wood-burning stoves; one we used for heat and the other Ma used for cooking. At least one of them was in use every day of the year, and because of this constant use, the enormous amount of black soot emitted into the air settled on everything, especially our papered walls. Almost on a yearly basis, we had to repaper them. Regardless of its physical appearance, this humble dwelling was a real home; a home filled with hard working people and a home filled with an abundance of love.

One of my fondest memories is Ma putting breakfast on our big, family-size table. We sat there with mouths watering for the taste of her hot biscuits and white sawmill gravy. Seated on hand-made splintery benches made from logs Pa cut down in the forest, we would impatiently lean our backs against a row of ill-fitting windows. On the other side of the glass were the rippling sounds of Irish Creek winding downward. Nobody cared, however, what was happening in the outdoor world because when my pa made his way to the head of that table, we knew Ma's hot biscuits were out of the oven *(I think I can taste one now)*.

This, I can tell you; that stream of water making its way to the valley below cut its bed through a portrait of beauty that only the hand of God could have painted. In the warm days of spring and summer, it was not uncommon to see a white-tailed deer bouncing through woodlands in search of a mate, or gray bushy-tailed squirrels sharpening their teeth on crumpled cones from towering pines. Bluebirds nesting in blossoming dogwoods, and robins in the nearby apple orchards sang to us in the mornings; chirping songs of crickets put us to sleep at night.

During the winter months at Montebello, things were quite different. When spring and summer passed away, the cold winds of winter prevailed. Layers of dense fog crept over the mountains and drifted downward to dissipate along the creek beds of the valley. From mid-December until the latter days of May, layers of snow frequently covered our doorsteps, and icicles dangled from the eaves of the roof.

For many, many years, from one generation to another, life in those parts of the Blue Ridge Mountains did not change. To be born there was to work there, and with little knowledge of what was going on in the world beyond, to die there. In the mid-teens of the twentieth century, families in this "neck of the woods" were large. A single day of work yielded but little pay. From one household to another, babies cried with hunger pangs while mothers searched their cupboards for enough flour and lard to bake a pan of biscuits and fill an iron skillet with gravy. There was no need to plan meals because they were always the same, milk gravy, dried fruit, potatoes, and beans.

Mountain boys became men at a young age. Working long backbreaking hours for six days a week taught us responsibility. How could I ever forget that day when Ma handed me a garden rake and told me to help in the garden? The rake was taller than I was, but I managed to handle it just the same. Early in the twentieth century, that is just the way things were. Even as kids, we worked before we played. When a new baby was born, parents saw the child, not as just another mouth to feed, but another pair of hands to work the land. If born a male, the child worked in either harvesting corn and hay or he went into the woods to cut timber. Females worked hard too. My sister, Hettie Mae, learned to cook and sew before she was *"knee high to a grasshopper"*.

A lumberjack's job is difficult and extremely dangerous. When rumors of World War I became reality, the men of Montebello were

Bob's Rabbits

some of the first to go and fight. I was still a lad when they left home, so I never knew much about the details of all that happened. You see, communications back then were not what they are today, especially in the heart of the Jefferson National Forest. I do know, however, that those men who stayed behind were few, and most of them did not fare much better than those who went to war.

Mostly what I remember about those years are the things I did when there were no chores, things like shooting colored

3

marbles and jumping stones in the creek. Once, I had a pen of white rabbits and raising them was quite a challenge, to say the least. I was young then, but I had fun caring for the cuddly pets. It was mostly in the summertime that I played outdoors because our winters were too harsh. In Rockbridge County, we did not have a tremendous amount of snow, but when we did, I loved pressing my nose against the icy windowpanes to watch the flakes as they gently fell. Almost nothing could pull me from that scene. In addition to the falling snow, I also remember all of those cold winter nights when the howling wind rattled our windows. That was when we buried ourselves beneath the weight of heavy hand-sewn quilts. Do you know how priceless these memories are? They are a treasure no one can take from you. We hold onto them forever.

Early in the twentieth century, education was not mandatory in Rockbridge County, and many children grew up illiterate. I was one of them. Ma wanted me to go to school, so when I turned six, she hustled me off with my older brothers. School, however, was a problem for me because I could not talk without stuttering. After a day or two of classes, older boys made fun of me, and I went home crying to my mother. "Well, just stay at home," she said. "I can use you here. You don't have to go back." I suppose one could say I was a first-grade dropout. As you can see, bullies did not arrive with the twenty first century. They have always been with us.

Certainly, those two days at school are not my best memories, but many of my childhood days are-especially holidays. Everybody in our lumber camp looked forward to Easter and Christmas, and to all of our quiet peaceful Sundays. Sunday mornings are some of my favorite memories. Neighbors and all of their kin met at the white framed church on top of the mountain. Some church meetings, especially those with singing, lasted an entire day. When that happened, the preacher excused the kids from afternoon meetings so we could play tag and hide-and-go-seek on the church grounds. As I look back on those times, I realize now what a tremendous impact Sunday church services made on my life. It was at church meetings people learned to care for one another. The bonding of hearts was the result of the time we shared together and that fellowship strengthened us spiritually. God also used those times for planting the seed of his word in our hearts. It is sad to know those Sundays are now gone.

Families forever mold our lives, and when my thoughts turn to family, I always think of my mother. She had the greatest influence on my life as a youngster. Ma was special to me. In fact, she was nothing less than precious. From the rising of the morning sun until it set beneath the lowest peaks of our mountains, she was hard at work. To me, she was beautiful, but lovelier than her pretty face with its piercing blue eyes, was the woman inside. She was one who never complained about anything. The love and concern she had for her family, especially her ability for spreading her love around, is what I remember most.

Pa and Ma

One cold and bitter winter when I was still very young, I came down with pneumonia. I cannot remember the year, but it may have been during the winter of the infamous Spanish flu. If so, I would have been six or seven years old. My mother sat by my bed night after night, wiping my feverish brow. Until she knew I was recovering, she rarely left my side. As I lay there listening to her sing, *"I Must Tell Jesus"*, I sensed the anxiety she felt for my wellbeing. Even though she had not yet experienced true salvation, *"I Must Tell Jesus"* was her song when there was trouble in our family. Years would pass before Ma truly knew the meaning of that old hymn.

My pa was special too. He was the perfect man for such a woman as my mother. While his wife and children toiled in the fields at home, he was hard at work doing multiple jobs for South River. Our mountains were steep, and the roads unpaved. To move the timber down to the valleys, it was loaded onto skids then pulled down the slopes by teams of horses and oxen. This work was dangerous, not only for men, but also for the animals. Many of them got hurt, and one of Pa's jobs was to care for injured horses.

Although he was an overseer for his company, Pa also cut and sold timber for himself. He had to do this to in order to care for his large family. I remember one year when we had to wait for him to cut and sell his chestnut timber before we could even buy our winter shoes.

In 1918-1919, when the tin mines were in operation, Pa also worked in the mines. Every workday, often before daybreak, he walked on foot over mountain trails to the woodlands. When his job was finished there, he came home and tended his farm. Sometimes, when harvesting tomatoes and beans for the canneries, Pa hired farmhands to help. While they took care of those two crops, his boys took care of corn and hay.

Irish Creek farmers also benefited from Pa's hard labor, and from his expertise in caring for farm animals. He doctored their cows and pigs, castrating them when needed; he also assisted them with the drenching of cows.

My memories of Pa and me together are many. The first coming to my mind is the time when he was helping the lumber company set railroad ties. One morning, he left home before daybreak, and after climbing half way up the mountain, he realized that he had forgotten his gloves. From atop the ridge, he yelled to Ma that he needed them. She handed me a lantern and told me to take the gloves to Pa. You should have seen me trying to get into that horse and buggy with a lantern in one hand and Pa's gloves in the other. I was just a little tyke and scared to death, but finally I was able to make it, and Pa got his gloves.

A second incident I recall with Pa was the day I helped him haul timber. We strapped two or three telephone pole timber to our horse drawn wagon, and then began to travel downhill on a steep mountain road. Pa told me to drive the horse while he acted as brakeman. Near the bottom of the mountain, we hit ice, and the wagon went out of control. It ran over my pa's foot, and then continued pushing the horse down the road. Pa yelled for me to stop the horse. He was in so much pain that all he could do was hold his crushed foot with both hands. Finally, when we reached a point where the road leveled, the horse went into a bank and halted. "Son," Pa called, "Remove the hooks from old John and bring him up here. If I can make it, we will try to get home." When it was all over, we learned Pa had a badly damaged foot, and that he would not be able to work for a long time. It was quite an experience for both of us.

Once, I had a very special day with Pa. It has to do with bringing the cow home. Every day at sundown, one of my older brothers went to the fields to bring in the cow, but on this particular day, the older boys were not at home. "Bob," my pa said, "see if you can't go out to the field and bring the cow in." Now, I was probably no more than five or six years old, so I was scared to death to go looking for that cow. Even so, whenever Pa told me to go, I went-no matter what. Parents in those days were not easy on their kids. They reared you to be tough, and because of this, you did not receive many compliments. Anyway, I went looking for the old cow. Finally, after a bit, I heard her bell ringing. She was in the woods, a right considerable distance from home. Although Bessie was much bigger than I was, I finally brought her home. Pa came to the barn to meet us. "Son," he said, "you did a good job. You will never know how proud I am of you."

I was proud too because it was not like Pa to brag on any of his kids. When he did, you knew you had done something special. He probably never knew how those remarks boosted my ego, but I have never forgotten the pride I felt that day.

Now, that I have told you about my family, you are probably wondering what role God played in our lives. As I previously stated, my family went to church every Sunday, but I cannot recall God ever having any place of significance in our home. I suppose I was just one of those kids who have ears but do not hear because Sunday church meetings were nothing more to me than having something to do. I am confident we had many true believers on Irish Creek, but within our household, we did not practice the Christian faith. There was no prayer, no Bible reading, or any time for worship at home. I believe, however, that even then, God was working in my life. Afterthought tells me it was He who gave us the strength and the will to survive. Our strong and healthy bodies, also given by him, prepared us for the leaner years that lay in the future.

Family

God made this earthly family especially for me
That I might always have a friend, and a friend to others be
He knew in bonds of family I could feel His loving touch
Moreover, from the day of birth, He loved me very much

7

My mother, gentle, kind and sweet, kept me in her care
While the armor for life's battles, my dad was proud to wear
Big brothers towering over me helped me find my way
And sisters never leave your side, no matter time of day
I'm grateful, Heavenly Father, for this home where I was placed
And one day in my final home, I'll thank You face to face

Chapter 02

The Folly of Fools

Sept.1928-Dec. 1930

. . . .

*"The wisdom of the prudent is to understand
his way; the folly of fools is deceit"*

By the time I was fourteen, I concluded those endless hours of farming and lumbering at Montebello were not for me, and so I left Irish Creek and went to live with my Aunt Annie in Stuarts Draft, Virginia. She agreed to give me room and board in exchange for work as a farm hand. Delighted that I would be on my own, there was little remorse when I said good-bye to the family. My departure, however, was not that easy for my mother. I can still see the tears trickling from the corners of her blue eyes. Nevertheless, I said farewell to her way of life.

Arriving at Aunt Annie's house, I deposited my rolled up overalls *(known today as blue jeans)* in the bottom drawer of a solid oak wardrobe. Outside the bedroom window, I could see the meadows were beginning to lose their green, and that the nearby orchard was more than ready for harvesting. Some of its fruit was scattered beneath the trees, and cascades of red and yellow apples clung to an army of broken branches now sweeping the ground. It was more than evident they needed to be gathered. Not wanting this gracious relative to have second thoughts about hiring me, I put on my cap, grabbed a stack of bushel baskets, and immediately went to work.

Three months after moving in with Aunt Annie, I turned fifteen. It was the week before Christmas, and I went home for the holidays. A gigantic bear hug from Pa greeted me at the door. Surviving Ma's wet kisses and a pinch to the nose, I sat down in her warm kitchen for a bowl of thick white potato soup. Nobody could make potato soup like Ma's-certainly not Aunt Annie.

"Mr. Sam wants to see you," Pa said as he sat down across from me at the table. "He asks about you every time I see him."

I picked up a cold biscuit spreading it heavily with apple butter. "Is that so?" I replied. "Mr. Sam always seemed to take a liking to me. When I was just a tyke, he would fill my pockets with licorice sticks, and then tell me that when I finished eating them I could come back for more. I'll have to drop by one day and see the old man."

That same afternoon, I decided to walk over to the Sam Miller farm. When I arrived, I saw him scurrying about the yard picking up trash. He must be expecting company, I thought as I opened the gate and entered his front yard. If he was not expecting someone, then the old man must have changed. For as far back as I could remember his place was always a mess.

"Well, young Bob Painter," Mr. Sam said as he came to greet me and shake my hand. "What a surprise! Come on in here, boy, and sit for a spell. We're having a little party come New Year's Eve and the wife's got me out here tidying up the place."

As I sat down on the porch steps beside our beady-eyed neighbor, I recalled his most notable talent. He could make the best cider on this end of the Blue Ridge. I grinned at the thoughts I was having, and at my aging friend. "If you're doing all this fixing up, Mr. Sam, you must be planning quite a party."

Mr. Sam chuckled. "Yep, he said. "I'm gonna have everybody around here come in for a dance."

"I reckon that means you made quite a bit of cider this year."

Sam spit tobacco juice over the splintered handrail where his stooped shoulders rested. "It's the most I ever made; lots of apples around here this year." He touched my shoulder. "I've got a deal for you, Bob. If you'll go visit my neighbors around here and invite them to this here shindig, I'll let you taste my cider."

"Is that for sure?"

"It's for sure," he promised.

For a moment, I wondered what Pa would do if he caught me drinking hard cider. Shucks, I said to myself, I'm making my own way in the world so why should I worry if Pa cares or not.

Mr. Sam must have read my thoughts because he raised his brow and looked straight into my eyes. "Do you think your pa would take to you drinking hard cider?"

I held my shoulders high, but my eyes stared at the ground around my boots. "I think I'm grown up enough now to make my own decisions about whether I'll drink, or not."

"Suit yourself, Son, but don't forget I asked you."

When I left the Miller farm, I promised Sam to be back just as soon as Christmas was gone.

The holiday went quietly. For gifts, there were red plaid flannel shirts or boots for the fellows and bright colored scarfs and knee socks for the girls. Ma was grateful for the new aprons my sisters made for her and Pa tried on his brown felt church hat a dozen times. All of us enjoyed the big thick peppermint candy sticks I found in Stuarts Draft, and one of my brothers came home with a mesh bag filled with oranges. A neighbor gave us a whole basket of black walnuts and a grocery bag filled with pecans.

When Ma called her family to come for dinner, we stuffed ourselves with a wild turkey Pa shot in the timberlands. Ma boiled parts of the bird for drippings that she turned into a huge pan of gravy. With her buttermilk biscuits, creamy mashed potatoes, and turnips confiscated from the cellar we had a feast. A big pan of bread pudding served as our dessert. Considering the year to be 1928, I suppose we had an excellent Christmas dinner.

Three days came and went. After twenty games of checkers and Pa winning fifteen of them, I was ready to get out of the house. I knew Mr. Sam was itching for me to tell everybody about his big party so just as soon as Pa laid down for an afternoon nap, I grabbed his jacket from the back of the kitchen door and headed for the Miller farm. As I made my way through the barren trees, the wind whipped at my back. My hands were freezing so I buried them deep within the pockets of the black wool coat and wished I had not forgotten to bring the gloves left behind at Aunt Annie's house.

When I was finally on the farm, the Millers were nowhere around. Patches of ice covered the tracks made by their horse and wagon. For a few minutes, I was a child again, slipping and sliding on the frozen tracks. Thin layers of ice sparkled on the barn's tin roof. Inside that barn, I surmised, would be the place where Mr. Sam might hide his cider. The very thought of taking my first drink was exciting, and the temptation to do so did not subside. You can be sure that I headed straight for that barn. While skidding down the icy pathway, I remembered what Pa once told me about apple cider when it freezes. "The alcohol flows right to the center of the barrel. If you really want to get drunk, just try drinking that stuff right from a barrel."

"How do you do that, Pa?"

"With a straw," he said. "Cider sipped through a straw is the best there is."

Keeping what Pa had told me in mind, I went in search of a dried milkweed to use for a straw. Not three minutes passed before I found a big patch of them behind Mrs. Miller's chicken coop. Every occupant in that building began to cackle, so I retrieved the longest reed I could reach and high-tailed it out of there. Holding the straw between my teeth, I made my way back to the barn and lifted the bolt on its big double doors. Inside the barn, stench from molded hay drifted from the loft above my head, and two lazy-looking cows lay side by side in stalls located on the right side. There were two more cattle stalls to my left, so the cider I decided, must be in the rear of the building.

As soon as I rounded the corner of the cows' stall, I spotted the wooden kegs hidden beneath layers of chicken wire and heavy logs. Uncovering one of the barrels, I pulled the cork out with my teeth. The sweet aroma of apple cider permeated the winter air. I pushed the milkweed quill into the icy slush.

I have no idea how long I stayed in that barn. I first thought it to be less than an hour, but I now believe it was much longer. I certainly was there long enough to drink myself into manhood, or perhaps I should say long enough to drink myself into a cold, drunken stupor. While still sitting on an empty keg where I had seated myself earlier, I heard the distant rumble of wagon wheels. Only then did I remember why I was there in the first place. Suppose the Millers found me and learned I had been into their brew before I went to tell the neighbors about the party. Most likely, old Sam would go into a rage. Plugging the keg, I stammered, "See you later, my friend."

Making my way from the barn, and with cold winter wind whipping at my back, I staggered along the pathway. I was warm-I mean very warm. While hustling away from the farm, I unbuttoned Pa's coat and headed for the nearest house. How I made it there, I will never know. My head was spinning like a top, and I could hardly stay on my feet. Finally, I collapsed by the side of the road and could go no further. Within seconds, I was out like a light.

"Bob Painter, what are you doing out here in such a condition as this? Your Pa's going to kill you when you get home."

It was the voice of Tom Williams, Pa's best friend.

"...you goin' to Mr. Sam's dance?" I asked.

"I'm going straight to your brothers. That's where I'm going."

"Go on," I muttered, "but Mr. Sam's gonna be real mad with ya."

Again, I passed out. The next time I opened my eyes two of my brothers were dragging me down the road.

When I was finally home, Pa only stared at me, but I knew from the look in his eyes, he was disappointed in my behavior. In the years to follow, I would recall many times how easy it is to take that first drink and how difficult it is to take the last.

After the cider-drinking incident, I returned to Aunt Annie's house, but before 1929 ended, I was once again restless. I needed money and working Aunt Annie's farm was not much income. I began to look for other employment and landed a job in a furniture factory. For the first time in my life, I knew how it felt to have money in my pockets. The *"jingle"*, however, was too good to last. Just as I was beginning to enjoy life, the Great Depression swept over the entire country, and as with millions of other people, my job was gone.

Within months, poverty was widespread, and in the Blue Ridge Mountains, bad times were at their worse. Because Pa could farm the land, my family fared better than most city folk; nevertheless, I needed a job for myself. I went to see Uncle John, Pa's older brother who owned a service station across the mountain in Waynesboro. After offering me a few weeks of work, he gave me a place to stay. A couple of months later, I went to visit my brother, Bernard, who lived in Roanoke County, more than 70 miles from Waynesboro.

Learning of my plight, my brother asked, "Why don't you come and live with me and the wife? On many days, I work the night shift, and Mildred is afraid when she is alone. You would be company for her."

I readily accepted Bernard's offer to move in with him and Mildred in Riverdale, *(now known as Grandview Heights).* With Roanoke City nearby, I should find a job. Hearing that Rocky Dale Stone Quarry needed help, I went and applied for a job and immediately, they hired me. Riverdale became home to me.

Still without God, I grew into manhood. As far as I was concerned, He did not exist. I lived only for pleasure. Not caring if it was right or wrong, I continued to drink liquor, smoke cigarettes, patronize movie houses, and care nothing about spiritual matters. My friends, my bottle, and a good time were all I needed.

After the move to Riverdale, I became obsessed with watching movies. All day long, on almost any Saturday, I made my rounds to Roanoke's theaters. Although God had no place in my life, I still realized that Hollywood is a sinful place. There is absolutely nothing in those movies to enhance one's mind. Today, they are far worse than in the 1930s and 40s. I am confident Hollywood lifestyles are the epitome of sin and degradation, and Christians should not watch that stuff. It does not help us one bit in our walk with God.

"For God so loved the world, that He gave his only begotten son,
that whosoever believeth in him should not
perish, but have everlasting life."

John 3:16

Chapter 03

Above Rubies

Jan. 1931-Aug. 1935

. . . .

"Who can find a virtuous woman? ...her price is far above rubies."

T he years of 1931 through 1934 were filled with poverty. Even in America's largest cities, people stood in soup lines, and jobs were scarce. From Riverdale, I continued to ride a bicycle for seven miles to my gruesome quarry job that paid almost nothing but room and board. It was depressing, to say the least, but sometimes we do what we have to do.

In Virginia, the summer of 1933 had been sizzling hot and dry, but in late September, those days were gone, at least in the Roanoke Valley. After an early frosty touch from autumn, the mountains surrounding us blazed with a multitude of colors. Having a day off from the quarry, I decided early in the morning to go fishing. Sitting on the banks of the Roanoke River that flowed through Roanoke City, I threw my line into the calm waters and relaxed against a maple that was, at that moment, so red it appeared to be on fire. Scanning its branches for the sight of a single bird or squirrel, I thought upon the magnificence of the seasons when one gives way to another. Only weeks ago those branches would have been clothed in forest green, and filled with crying blue jays. That day, the green was gone and a pillow of red filled its space. Squirrels I normally saw around the river's banks were gone too. Supposedly, the blasts from hunters' guns had scared them all away.

I jiggled the fishing pole and continued to wait for my first catch of the day. Turning my thoughts from the beauty surrounding me, I wondered about the purpose for it all-the earth-the seasons-me. Many questions taunted me. There was absolutely nothing in my life of any significant importance. Part of me was alive and well, but part of me was dead. Something was definitely missing. Little did I realize that this missing link was a man whose name is Jesus.

Not a nibble did I feel on the other end of my line. Lifting my rod, I checked the bait. The worm was still fighting for its life. Thinking this to be a perfect day to catch a brim, or possibly a big catfish, I cast my line downstream. Nothing happened, not even one bite. Finally, after repeatedly moving from one fishing hole to another, I decided that absolutely this was not a good day for fishing. Pulling my rod from the water, I discarded the bait, wrapped the line around the pole, and then tucked the gear beneath one arm. Grabbing the box of fishing lures, I headed for home.

Shuffling through a sea of fallen leaves, I continued my reflections on life, especially did I ponder on the beauty of this autumn day. A frightened squirrel darted across the road then scampered up an aging oak that was still holding its leaves. At that moment, I decided to take a detour from the main road. Turning onto a well-trodden path, I walked several feet, and then looked up. An enormous flock of geese flew over my head, all of them honking in unison. I stopped to watch them in flight, and that is when I saw her.

Ginny

Even though she was bending over a basket filled with curly kale, I saw that she was tall and stately. I watched closely while she cut the stems from another sprout, tossing it onto the over-flowing container. She did not know I was there. When the basket would not hold another salad leaf, she stood erect, and though she appeared to be a bit shy, I thought she was just about the prettiest girl I had ever seen. Not bad, I said to myself, not bad at all.

Suddenly, the young woman realized I was watching her. Turning her body so that I no longer could see her face, she propped the basket upon her right hip and climbed a nearby embankment. I continued to stare until she had disappeared down the other side.

"Bernard," I said to my brother when arriving home a few minutes later, "I just saw a girl out in a garden picking greens, and I'd sure like to get a date with her."

"Where did you see her?"

"On a farm, down the road apiece."

"Oh, that must have been Virginia Morgan. She's Howard Morgan's sister."

"He's never told me about any sister," I replied. "...wonder why?"

"Well, I don't know, but if you're so interested in her, ask him."

"Yeah, I will the next time I see him."

Although Howard was the first friend I made after moving to Riverdale I had never been to his house, but I certainly had no intentions of waiting until I saw him again to ask about his good-looking sister. The next evening I found a reason to pay him a visit. My knees were trembling when I walked up the walkway to the Morgan home. I hesitated for a moment, and then gently knocked on the front door. To my delight, Virginia opened the door. My heart began to sing. Something strange was happening to me.

"Hello," she said. "My name is Ginny. May I help you?"

"Is Howard home?" I asked.

"What's up, Bob?" asked my friend who suddenly appeared from out of nowhere.

For the life of me, I could not remember what I had planned to say. "I-I-I'm just messing around," I stammered, "and thought I'd drop by and see what you were up to."

"Well, come on in and have a seat. I've got milking to do right now, but you and Ginny can talk until I get back, that is, unless you want to go with me."

"Naw, I don't think so," I responded, wondering if he thought I was stupid enough to pass up this opportunity to be with his sister. Howard excused himself and left the parlor, closing the door as he went. I was alone with Ginny.

"Where do you live?" Ginny asked when her brother was gone.

"...Up the road. Do you know Bernard and Mildred Painter?"

"I've heard of them, but you know how it is in a neighborhood like this. You hear people's names, but you don't actually know them."

"Yeah, I do know. That's the way it is back at home. I'm Bernard's brother, and we come from over in Rockbridge County."

For some time, the conversation was nothing more than idle chitchat. I told her about the latest movie I had seen, and she responded to me as if she could not care less about the movie or its infamous star. I was expecting to hear her rave on and on about Cary Grant, the heartbeat of most young women, but she just continued to listened to me. Later, I learned that she was not nearly as interested in movies as I was.

"By the way," she addressed me when there seemed to be nothing else to talk about, "Do you go to church with your brother?"

Shaking my head, I answered, "No. Bernard doesn't go to church. I use to go with my family, but I haven't been to church since leaving home. Why did you ask me that? Do you go?"

For a minute, her mind appeared to go blank. "I'm sorry," she said. "Do I what?"

"Go to church? You asked me if I went to church, so now I'm asking you if you go."

"Oh, yes, I do. We all go to Riverdale Baptist."

It did not take me long to know what my next question would be, and I could hear my excitement speaking for me. "Are you going Sunday?"

"Well, this week we can't go on Sunday morning, but we're going Sunday night."

I suppose I should have asked her why she was not going on Sunday morning, but it made no difference to me if it was morning, noon or night; I simply wanted to be with her. Hoping she was not going to come up with an excuse, I looked downward and asked sheepishly, "Do you think I could tag along?"

"Well, I suppose so. I mean anybody can go to church, can't they?"

Wow! We had a date. It was just what I had come here to do, and she was the one that knew how to do it.

At that moment, Howard returned from his milking. The three of us spent another hour talking about nothing. For the full sixty minutes, I was wishing Howard would leave again, but it did not happen. During that time, Mrs. Morgan came into the parlor, and Ginny introduced us. "Bob's going to church with us Sunday night," Ginny said. "Is that okay?"

"Of course," her mother replied. "We'll take all of the folks we can get."

Mrs. Morgan excused herself and left the room. "I'd better go," I said to Howard. "I don't want to wear out my welcome. Drop by one evening and we'll take in a movie."

"Sure enough," he replied as he showed me to the door. Ginny remained seated on the sofa while I lingered long enough to wave at her. She was smiling, so I think that even then she liked me a bit.

I was on *"pins and needles"* for the rest of that week-certain that something was going to happen to cause Ginny to cancel our date. Several times, I was tempted to go and see her again, but knowing it was not the proper thing to do, I refrained.

Sunday evening finally arrived, and I borrowed a shirt and tie from Bernard so I would be properly dressed for the service. As Ginny and I walked from her house to the church, I wondered if she could hear my heart pounding. I wanted to reach out and take hold of her hand, but decided that might not be the right thing to do just yet.

When we arrived at the church, Ginny smiled as she introduced me to some of her friends. We settled ourselves on the very back pew, and for the first time in my life I knew that I was going to enjoy being in church. Although I knew I should not do it, I constantly whispered to the wonderful girl sitting beside me. About halfway through his sermon, the pastor, whose last name was also Painter, stopped speaking. "Young man," he said while looking straight at me, "you either stay quiet while I'm preaching or get up and leave." I was so embarrassed, and so fearful that the Morgans would never allow me to see Ginny again that I remained quiet throughout the remainder of the service.

In later years, the minister, Rev. K.A. Painter, reminded me of that incident. Often, he would say to me, 'I know somewhere along the line, we are kin'. If we were, we never learned how.

Ginny's parents did allow me to see her again, and more often than I ever dreamed. I knew she liked me, and I more than liked her. We began double dating with Ethel Chisom and Gerald Atkins, two of Ginny's friends. Immediately, Gerald and I became pals. One Sunday night, neither of us had cigarettes, so while our girlfriends were at church the two of us headed for a local bar to purchase a couple of packs of Camels. We arrived at the bar early in the evening, and the temptation to have a beer was far too difficult to resist so we began drinking. By closing time, both of us were "plastered". As we staggered back to our houses, somebody apparently spotted us because when morning came we learned we were a disgrace to the whole community. I was more than ashamed of my behavior, and I was certain Ginny would never forgive me. Much to my surprise, she barely mentioned it. Later, I discovered her father to be somewhat of a social drinker, so I suppose she already knew what alcohol does to its users.

Ginny and I saw each other as often as possible, and before we realized how quickly time passes, an entire year was gone. Life could not have been better for us when suddenly, our world turned upside down. The first bombshell to hit was a lay-off at the quarry, and then to complicate matters, Bernard purchased a farm in Botetourt County, moving his family from Riverdale to Fincastle, twenty-one miles from Riverdale and Ginny. Madly in love, both of us were devastated. We vowed that the move would not prevent us from being together. For a brief period, I found work with the state highway department, but it did not last and I was out of work again. The Norfolk and Western Railway then hired me, but that job also played out.

On weekends, whenever Bernard had to work, I rode with him from Fincastle to the American Viscose plant. I then walked the remaining two miles to see Ginny. When my brother did not have to work, I chose to walk the entire twenty-one miles. Once, I even walked the distance during a winter ice storm. With nothing covering my feet but a thin pair of socks and leather shoes, my feet were almost frozen. The ice was so deep it cut into my ankles. Ginny's brothers laughed at me for being so foolish, but I loved my girl and nothing was going to prevent me from being with her. I was confident that she loved me as much as I loved her, and not caring how Mr. and Mrs. Morgan would react, I pressed Ginny to get married.

"I don't think so, Bob," she said repeatedly. "How would we live without any income?"

In my heart, I knew Ginny was right to refuse me, but I wanted her for my own more than I had ever wanted anything in my life. Finally, I decided if I did not stop the persuasion, I was going to lose her. Several weeks passed, and then on a beautiful Sunday afternoon, Mr. Morgan and Ginny gave me a ride to Fincastle. As we turned into Bernard's driveway, a young girl from the neighborhood, Tiny Minnix, ran behind the house. I knew Ginny saw her, and after we were in Bernard's living room, she gave me the silence treatment. There was no mention of Tiny. Ginny just simply remained quiet for the remainder of the time we had together.

The following weekend, one of those when I walked to Riverdale, I had barely stepped inside the Morgan's house when my beautiful, timid Virginia profusely pounced on me. "Who was that girl at your house last week?"

Immediately, I saw jealousy. "Tiny Minnix," I answered.

I saw Ginny's bottom lip quiver as she began biting it. "What was she doing there?"

"...just visiting Mildred. Why?"

"Well, why did she leave in such a hurry-as if she didn't want me to see her?"

I chuckled to myself. This was to be my moment. I walked over to her, lifted her chin, and then put my arms around her. Peering straight into her eyes, I whispered, "When are you going to marry me?"

"I don't know," she stammered. "I mean, I'm not sure."

Silence abounded. She was still thinking about Tiny-wondering if there was something that she did not know. I kept staring at her until she spoke again. "When do you want me to marry you?"

Quickly, before she could change her mind, I replied, "How about next Saturday?"

Before she could respond to that, she took a very deep breath. "Okay; we'll do it, but only if nobody knows."

I thought I must have been dreaming. Ginny, the most wonderful girl on the face of the earth had just consented to marry me-me, the kid from Irish Creek who did not even have a job. If only the marriage could be today!

"You'll never be sorry," I promised her as we made plans for the following weekend.

The next five days were the longest ones in my life. Ginny and I had decided we would meet at the market square in downtown Roanoke. Mr. Morgan would be selling wood on the market so Ginny would catch a ride with him. From Fincastle, I would ride to town with a neighbor who also sold goods on the market. Repeatedly we cautioned each other to be careful so that neither man would know our plan.

Ginny and Me

Our wedding day was August 3, 1935, and it was a sizzling hot day. We met on the market square at Turners' Drug Store. From there, we caught a city bus to Salem, the county seat. "Do you really think we should do this?" Ginny asked on the ride to the courthouse.

"We'll work things out...I promise."

In the clerk's office, an aging woman sat leisurely at her desk. When she arose to greet us, I squeezed Ginny's arm.

"How old are you?" The woman asked me.

"Twenty-one," I replied.

The clerk looked at Ginny. "How old are you?" Ginny did not answer.

Again, the clerk asked for Ginny's age. When she again refused to answer, the woman grinned. "I understand," she said, and then looked at me. "Robert, your license will be one dollar."

As we made our way to a nearby Methodist church, I was clutching the license in one hand and holding Ginny's arm with the other. After entering the building, we found the elderly pastor, Rev. Murray D. Mitchell sitting by a window looking out. He never asked why we were there, just greeted us both, and then shook my hand. Apparently, he assumed we had come to be married.

"What's your name," asked the minister?

"Robert Painter."

"What about her?"

"She's Virginia Morgan."

With a twinkle in his eye, the old man pushed himself up from the chair. Then, as though a marriage was nothing more than a matter of business, he extended an opened hand then spoke again. "Let me have the license and follow me."

There was not another question-no witnessing-no counseling-not anything. We simply walked into the sanctuary where the minister mumbled a few ceremonious words and then pronounced us man and wife. "Be good to her," he said to me, and with those four little words of advice, he smiled at Ginny, and then shook my hand. I nodded in agreement.

I reached into my trousers' pocket for the few dollars I had made while working for Bernard. "How much do I owe you?" I asked.

"Three dollars"

"Three dollars," I muttered. Three dollars was three days' pay, an awful lot of money when I did not even have a job. Although I thought the fee was far too much money for such a simple ceremony, I handed the money to him. I was simply too happy to voice a complaint.

There was no honeymoon and no celebration of any kind. When we left the church, Ginny went home with her dad; I went back to Fincastle.

For two or three weeks, I went to see Ginny for our usual weekend dates. We were confident that no one knew about our marriage. Then, it all came to a head. One Saturday morning when I arrived at the house, Mrs. Morgan came to the door. "You rascal," she said. That was all I needed to hear. Our secret marriage was no longer a secret.

I looked at my wife. "She knows?" I inquired.

"Everybody knows," Ginny said. "It came out in the newspaper."

"I knew before then," Mrs. Morgan piped. "Your license fell from its hiding place behind my photograph." She grabbed my shoulders. "You had better tell her Daddy about it."

When Mr. Morgan came home, I was nervous. Anxiously, I took him aside. "Do I have your permission to marry Ginny?" I asked.

The man looked at me with a frown, never responding to my question. I was too frightened to ask the second time. Later that night, after they were in bed, Mrs. Morgan told her husband the marriage had already taken place. I am told he jumped out of the bed, as mad as a hornet, but by the time I arrived the following Saturday, on behalf of Ginny, he had reconsidered. I knew Mr. Morgan liked me, but when I saw him standing in the opened doorway, my knees trembled. "I know you and Ginny are married," he said, "so as long as you're not working, you might as well move in here with us and help me cut wood."

Mr. Morgan's response to our marriage was difficult for me to believe. In less time than was needed for me to snap my fingers, he had offered me a home. My shoulders dropped and my heart nearly stopped beating. This was a blessing that I did not deserve.

Chapter 04

So Great a Salvation

Sept.1935-Jan. 1942

. . . .

"How shall we escape if we neglect so great salvation; ..."

No two people could be more opposite than Ginny and me. I am outgoing, talkative, impulsive, persuasive, and a risk taker. The best way to describe Ginny is to say that she is calm, cool, and collected. She has great powers of observation and is very artistic; as are most women, she is also highly intuitive. She keeps both of her feet on the ground. Those who know us well say she follows along behind me and picks up the pieces. I suppose we complement one another with our differences.

Ginny's family was a large family, just as many were in those days. Joel and Cora Morgan's children included Claude, Howard, Virginia, Dora, and Robert Eugene *(Gene)*. Because Ginny and I lived with them for so long, I think I became like a son.

During the early years of our marriage, Papa *(as Ginny and I called her dad)*, Howard, and I loved to coon hunt on Saturday nights. While the women listened to the Grand Ole Opry, the men high tailed it off to the woods. Sometimes, we went there more to drink booze than to hunt coon. In those days, that is when most men drank their booze, either out in the barn, or while hunting and fishing with other men. Since Cora never approved of any alcoholic beverages, Papa was not too much of a drinker. I really think he drank with us so we would not think him to be anti-social. Although I cannot speak for Mr. Morgan, I am confident that if it were not for the intervention of God and his marvelous grace, that with those hunting trips and other drinking sprees I enjoyed, I would have become an alcoholic beyond repair.

Ginny and I had only been married a few weeks when she found a job with Puritan Mills, a Roanoke sewing factory. Shortly thereafter, the stone quarry recalled me. Franklin Roosevelt was President then, and the nation was slowly emerging from the depression. As did all families during this recovery period, we struggled to make ends meet.

Layoffs seemed to be the story of my life. Two years later, after Ginny and I were on our own, I was laid-off again. This time the job loss was in my best interest. The American Viscose Company, a leading employer in The Roanoke Valley, was taking applications. I applied for a job and fortunately, they hired me. In 1937, wages were low in the Roanoke area so when I received my first paycheck and we saw how much I made, Ginny and I were elated. Immediately, we purchased our first automobile, a 1935 Plymouth. By today's standard, we were still poor, but after the deep poverty of my childhood, and the struggles we had experienced since the day we were married, I did not feel poor at all.

On January 2, 1938, God blessed our home with our first little girl and we named her Joyce Darlene. Like all fathers with their first child, I thought she was the prettiest baby on the face of the earth. She most certainly was the joy and pride of my life. After Joyce's birth, Ginny did not return to her job at the mill. With a good wife, a job, a beautiful baby girl, and excellent health, I should have been thankful. I did not deserve the blessings God gave me, and just like most sinners, I never thanked him for anything. My only desires were for whatever benefited me, and my family.

The months passed swiftly and work at the rayon plant became very unstable. First, I was working, and then I was not. It was like having a part-time job. During one of the lay-off periods, I heard of a government program that would teach trades to the unemployed. I applied for the training and became an electric welder. The welding school was my only formal education and I never once used the skills I learned. Eventually, I did leave the American Viscose with more than 10 years of service.

Finally, the country's leaner years of the thirties were gone and jobs became more plentiful. Having a little money in my pocket, I drank more booze, smoked my cigarettes, chewed tobacco, gambled, and patronized all of the movie houses. Other than the devotion I had for my family, my life counted for almost nothing.

Late in 1941, Ginny and I began to make plans for Joyce's fourth birthday that was coming up in January of 1942. Since I loved movies so much, and Joyce had never seen one, we decided to take her to see *"Gone with the Wind"*. The movie opened in Roanoke during the early days of December so that meant we would celebrate her birthday a month early. On Sunday, December 7, we went to the theater. After purchasing popcorn for the three of us, I reminded Joyce that she would have to stay quiet; if she did not, we would have to leave. The news was just beginning when we took our seats. Suddenly, there came an announcement, the Japanese had bombed Pearl Harbor and all military men were to report to their bases immediately. Ginny and I gasped in disbelief, and Joyce spilled all of her popcorn. Quietly, everyone left the theater. That is, all were quiet except our little girl.

Joyce Darlene

"I didn't mean to spill the popcorn," Joyce sobbed. "I promise to be good."

No one was listening to her pleading.

Out on the streets of Roanoke, everyone was in shock. Even though we were strangers to one another, we talked and cried at the same time. Joyce, because she thought she had caused the ruckus that made her mama and daddy cry, was more upset than anybody. She had never seen us in tears.

The days to follow December 7 were very sober times in American history. Ginny's brothers, Claude and Howard were both in the military. When they had to return to their bases, the Morgan family was very upset. Although Mrs. Morgan, Ginny, and Dora would not allow their

27

emotions to show, when the boys were gone, their tears took over. Joyce did not know what was going on, so she retreated to a big rock in the front yard and sat with her hands over her ears. Ginny and I never knew about this until Joyce told us about it many years later.

The following Saturday, I went to the same theater as the week before to see *"The Call of the Wild"*. How little did I know then that I would never see another film made in Hollywood?

Christmas of 1941 was a sad holiday for the entire world. We were at war, and all across the country, Americans were celebrating the holiday in fear. Although alcohol never solves anybody's problems, and most certainly cannot win a war, men will still turn to a bottle instead of turning to God. In the Roanoke Valley, even at the onset of war, that is exactly what we did. On Christmas Eve, Papa Morgan and I celebrated the season by brewing up a large batch of extremely wicked eggnog. By evening, we did not know if we were coming or going because both of us were as drunk as a dog. Was Ginny mad? No, she was more than mad, and she let me know it by pouring my entire bottle of eggnog down the kitchen drain. Of course, this sent me into a drunken rage. With a few chosen words, I slapped her across the face, and she went crying to her daddy. When he learned why I had slapped her, his response to her was 'Hush, girl. If you poured my liquor down the drain, I would beat you to a pulp'.

Throughout that evening, Ginny and I fought like cats and dogs. Our little girl was one week from being four years old, and there I was, beating up on her mother because of a bottle of liquor. For the next several days, I carried a heavy burden of guilt. My sins were tearing me apart, and I did not know which way to turn. I know now that God was working in my life.

On the Sunday night following Christmas Day, I heard a sermon on the radio by Rev. Charles E. Fuller, from Long Beach, California. He preached a powerful message on the second coming of Jesus Christ. The Holy Spirit tugged heavily on my heart. The more I thought about my soul lost in eternity the more burdened I became. One night during that week I had a dream about the *"rapture"*, and in it, I went to heaven. When I told Ginny about the dream she laughed, and laughed, and laughed. "Robert, you'll never go to heaven, not in a million years," she jeered. That remark only caused me to reflect more on how I was living.

The following week, our Plymouth's dashboard light went out, so on Saturday morning I drove it to Hayden Brothers in Vinton to have it repaired. "It will be a little while," said the mechanic, "before I can replace it, but if you want to wait, there are chairs in the front office."

After spitting juice from a plug of Red Coon tobacco, I walked into a small room at the front of the garage. A short, balding man sat in one of two straight-back chairs. As I pulled the second one over to a blazing potbelly stove in the corner of the room, the man smiled at me and asked, "Have you heard that fellow preach over here at Midway?"

"Who's that?" I asked.

"The name's Fred Garland. He is about the best preacher I have ever heard. Before he got converted, he was on dope and everything else, even spent some time in Sing-Sing."

"Is that right?" I sat backwards in the chair with my chin resting on the top slat. "How long is he going to be preaching there?"

"Through next week, I hear. He's holding a revival for Midway Christian, and by the way, he comes from Roanoke... grew up in Southeast."

"Well, how 'bout that? I might just go over there tonight and see what he has to say. ...appreciate you telling me about him."

Still feeling guilty about the Christmas Eve incident, the stranger's talk about an evangelist rescued from a world of drugs only brought more conviction to my heart. I asked him a number of questions about the revival, including the location of the church and the time services would begin. The more the man talked, the more I wanted to hear. By the time the mechanic came for me, I had made up my mind-I was going to that meeting.

That evening, instead of going to the theater as I usually did, I went alone to Midway Christian Church. When I walked inside, a lot of activity and talking was going on among the people. I knew from the packed pews that Fred Garland must be quite a speaker. Since I was a stranger, I took a seat near the rear of the auditorium. At the front of the room, several men chatted with one another. I wondered which of them was Garland. Promptly at seven, one of them got up from his seat and walked to the podium. He introduced himself as the pastor of Midway, and then announced that Fred Garland was ill and would not be preaching. People gasped, and whispers spread among the congregation. I was furious. I gave up a good movie to come here, and now the man I came to hear wasn't even going to preach. I felt like leaving.

I can no longer remember the evangelist's first name, but the substitute for Fred Garland was a young man whose last name was Morris. Actually, I do not remember much about the service, but I know God's reason for sending me there. When the song service ended, the young preacher came to the podium with an opened Bible spread across his hands. "My text tonight is *How Shall We Escape if We Neglect So Great Salvation*. Please turn to the book of Hebrews, the second chapter."

Of course, since I did not read, I did not have a Bible. At the onset of the message, the Holy Spirit began speaking to me. I don't remember much about what Brother Morris had to say, but by the time the invitation was given, I wanted to know this Jesus, who being the Son of God, was willing to be made lower than the angels so He could die for me. I moved out of the pew and down the aisle where I fell to my knees. There among strangers, on January 29, 1942, I became a new creation in Christ Jesus. God truly wrought a miracle in my heart. When I left that church, I was a different person. Ginny, I thought, is not going to believe what has happened to me this night.

Two days passed. I did not tell Ginny about my salvation because I knew she was going to take it lightly, and when I did tell her, that is exactly what happened. I suppose she thought I was trying to cover up for the fights I provoked on Christmas Eve, or maybe it was because she had not yet experienced the transformation that takes place when one is born into God's family. I asked her to attend the revival services with me, and she refused. Finally, after pleading with her, she consented to go with me.

When Ginny and I attended that first meeting together, Fred Garland had returned, and by the time the revival services ended, my wife was under deep conviction. On the final night of revival, Joyce began to cry during the service. I carried her outside and walked to a nearby barn.

Looking up, I prayed aloud, "Lord, Ginny's got to get saved. Please, make it happen tonight."

Ginny did not accept the Lord that night, but when Fred Garland closed the meeting, he closed it with these words, "Just let go, and surrender your all to God."

The next day was Monday, and always in those years, Monday was laundry day for the women folk. Still under deep conviction, Ginny was hanging clothes on the backyard line. Finally, she could no longer withstand the pressure from the Holy Spirit. Remembering those final words from Sunday night, she threw a sheet over the fence and fell to her knees. "Okay, God," she cried, "I surrender. If you want me, I'm yours."

 "Beginning Again"

I know of a place called the "old rugged cross"
By way of "Beginning Again"
It's the place you and I may go anytime
And be freed from the burden of sin

We find at the cross, the depths of God's grace,
For mercy drops fall from above
All the judgment we fear, every heartache and tear
Are lost in the arms of His love

Like tattered old garments left by the door,
Never again to be worn
God takes the blame, our guilt, and our shame,
And remembers them not any more

Chapter 05

Grace that is Greater

Feb. 1942-Dec. 1942

. . . .

"Grace! Grace! God's Grace! Grace that is greater than all my sin"

When February of 1942 arrived, Ginny and I were two brand new Christians and the United States was fighting a raging war. All around us, people lived in a state of fear, never knowing if the war would escalate and come to American shores. I wondered if God could use me to help them. I cannot speak for my wife, but as for me, I knew my heart was changed. Immediately after my salvation, the Holy Spirit began to bring conviction to my heart. Because of the passion I had for them, the movies were the first worldly attraction to go. I never went to see another one, and I have never had a television in my home. This may seem far-fetched to those of this twenty-first century who have two or three T.V.s in their homes, but it has been a long-lasting conviction of my heart. I believe Hollywood and television to be one of the most destructive tools Satan has used to destroy the morals of this once great nation.

I was in love again; this time I was in love with Jesus. God took a rotten, sinful soul and turned it into a useful vessel, fit for his service. I could not hear enough of His precious words. Every night, I washed dinner dishes so Ginny could read the Bible to me. The more I heard, the more I wanted to know. I loved every word she read, but my heart was so hungry for truth, I knew I had to read for myself. Repeatedly,

I called upon the Lord. "Dear God," I prayed, "I cannot learn when I cannot read. Please help me to learn."

One evening while Ginny was clearing the dinner table, I walked into the living room, picked up the Bible and took a seat on the sofa. Opening the book, I looked down. *Romans*, I read at the top of the page. *Chapter 6*, I read again. Now, how can I possibly know I am in the book of Romans at Chapter 6? I read the next line aloud. *"What shall we say then?"* Is that how that line really reads, I wondered?

"Ginny," I called to my wife who was now at the kitchen sink. "Come here! You will not believe what has happened."

My wife peered at me from the doorway. "Robert, what are you up to?"

I held the Bible out to her. "Read to me the first five words on this page."

Drying her hands on the ruffled apron she was wearing, Ginny took the Bible and sat down beside me. *"What shall we say then?"* she read.

"I read that," I said to her. "I read those same words exactly as you read them. Honey, God is allowing me to read! He has answered my prayers!"

"Bob, are you crazy? You know you cannot read."

"But, I can. Give me the Bible and I will read you the next lines."

She handed it to me, and I again pointed my finger to verse one. *"What shall we say then? Shall we continue in sin, that grace might abound? God forbid. How shall we that are dead to sin, live any longer therein?"*

"Robert Painter, just stop right there."

Ginny was losing patience with me.

"You are repeating those lines from somebody's sermon. Give me that Bible and I will find you something to read that you have not heard."

She grabbed my Bible, flipped through the pages, and then handed it back to me. "Here," she said with her finger on a line in the first verse. "Read this."

The page heading told me it was the Book of Proverbs, and she was pointing to Chapter 20, verse 1.

Again, I read aloud. *"Wine is a mocker, strong drink is raging: and whosoever is deceived thereby is not wise."*

"That is exactly what it reads," Ginny said, "and you should know as well as anybody how true that verse is."

I twitched my nose at her and disregarded the remark because I knew she was trying to tease me. "All I know," I retorted, "is that God is teaching me to read, so just go on back to the kitchen and wash your dishes."

My wife did not leave the room. Instead, she leafed through the pages of the Bible, going from one verse to another, and finally, she was convinced that something strange had happened to me. Without missing a word, I read every passage of scripture she put before me.

There is no doubt in my mind that on that very day, God performed a miracle in my life. I wholeheartedly believe this because to this day I cannot spell, and I cannot write except to sign my name. God answered the prayers of a searching heart, and I could not lay His Book down. Day after day, week after week, I hungered to know more. The more I learned, the more I wanted to share it with others, and the more I grew in the Lord, the more I wanted victory over my sins.

Alcohol was a problem for me, but not as much as the tobacco. I struggled long and hard with these two convictions. I wanted ever so much to quit smoking, and Satan constantly fought me on the matter. One day while working at the viscose plant, I asked permission for a break. My boss was reluctant to give me relief because I had already taken a break. I knew that if I didn't get alone with God, I was going to go crazy, and so I requested again to be relieved. Finally, the supervisor sent someone to cover my assignment. I looked around for a place where I could be alone, and in a room where we washed sulfuric acid from the yarn, I found a pile of wet rayon waste. There, I fell down and cried out to my Heavenly Father. I told Him that I could not give up the alcohol and cigarettes, that if He did not want me using them then He would have to take away my desire for them. Then, and there, He answered my prayer. From that moment onward, I never had a desire for tobacco or alcohol in any form. Such moments as this one are the times God taught me about the power He has to offer his children. When we stop trying to work things out on our own, cast all of our cares upon Him, then He does some miraculous things.

I thank God for the help I received from fellow Christians. At the workplace, my boss thought I was losing my mind, and said so. "Not Bob," said Richard Hamrick, a fellow co-worker, "He's just got a little of what we need a whole lot of."

Another co-worker, Rev. Tommy Hillman, pastor of Gravel Hill Baptist Church, became my mentor. Together, we had daily Bible studies, and he answered many of my questions. This man was probably the most influential person I have had in my spiritual growth.

Winter passed, the war continued, and spring of 1942 arrived as beautiful as always in the Shenandoah Valley. Apple trees blossomed in the orchards, robins built nests in the spreading oaks, and purple iris blossomed in the city parks. I was still a new Christian, but I felt strongly that God was calling me to preach. He opened doors I could have never opened.

One Sunday morning, May 5, 1942, just five months after my salvation, I had the opportunity to give my personal testimony at Jordantown Wesleyan Methodist Church. When the altar call was given, a number of souls accepted Jesus. These were my first converts, and I never knew the name of even one, but it really does not matter, does it? In heaven, we will all have new names.

Not long after that meeting, I witnessed to a man whose last name was Cash, and he became my first single convert. I once knew his first name, but I cannot remember it now. In those war years of the forties, souls were searching for God, and they readily responded to the gospel. After the Cash conversion, there were just too many converts to count.

During this time, evangelistic meetings took place all over the city of Roanoke and Ginny and I attended most of them. I well remember the revival at Red Hill Baptist Church with Dr. Charles Stevens. Later, he became the founder of Piedmont Bible College. There were also several revival services at the City Market Auditorium in Roanoke and Brother J. H. Mason also held great services at the Christian Missionary Alliance Church. I was growing in the Lord and wanted to do everything within my power to win others.

I also closely followed the ministry of Evangelist Fred Garland. One night I went to him and told him I knew of a place in Riverdale where he could put his tent. He was more than interested in checking the place out, and after doing so, scheduled a revival for the neighborhood. The tent was finally set up and services were just about to begin when a windstorm blew up and ripped the tent apart. Why did this happen? Nobody could understand why God allowed this to happen, but because God was saving so many souls through Fred Garland's ministry, I am convinced it was the work of the old devil. I was still confident God wanted the gospel preached in Riverdale, so I determined in my heart that I would not be discouraged.

"But they that wait upon the Lord shall renew their strength;
they shall mount up with wings of eagles; they shall run
and not be weary; and they shall walk and not faint."

Isaiah 40:31

Chapter 06

Sowing in Tears

Jan.1943- Dec.1943

. . . .

"They that sow in tears shall reap in joy."

In 1943, World War II was still ravishing our allies across the Atlantic, and people around the world lived in fear of where the next battle might be. Here in the United States, many families suffered the loss of loved ones who went to fight, but the sting of that war as it was felt by other countries was never felt by most of us. We did find food items, such as coffee and sugar to be rationed, and sometimes not even available. Gasoline was also one of those commodities. Because of the gasoline shortage, Ginny and I were unable to visit with Ma and Pa who were still at Irish Creek. Once, while I was working for the Norfolk and Western Railway, I was able to get two free passes for a train ride. Ginny wrote Ma informing her that Joyce and I were coming to visit. When we arrived in Vesuvius, the mail carrier met us and gave us a ride up the mountain to Montebello. His stops at every mailbox irritated me, but Joyce found them to be exciting. When we returned the same way, we had to get up before daylight to catch a ride back down the mountain. After that single trip, we did not see Pa and Ma for a long time. A couple of times I tried making the trip by car, but once, the radiator overheated, and the second time, the battery died. In both instances, we had to return home.

While the war continued to take its toll around the world, Christians in America were ripe for revival and sinners were in search of a Savior. At any given church meeting, one might see a dozen souls kneeling at an altar. More and more, I sought God's will for my life, but because I was so illiterate, I saw no way possible for Him to use me. I had a heart burdened to preach the Word, but how could God use a "nobody" from the backwoods of Virginia? I could not even write a love note to my beloved wife.

The burden I carried for the people of Riverdale continued to haunt me. There were only three people in the neighborhood that I knew went to church-Mrs. Doran, Mrs. Chambers and Mr. Grubbs. Nevertheless, God impressed upon my heart to build an open-air tabernacle. To do that would not be easy, but I had to start somewhere. Finally, I decided to ask for help. Day after day, I walked from house to house, knocking on doors and sharing my burden with the lost community. All I wanted was a roof with four posts to hold it. By July, I had raised more than $1,300. Mr. Velty Wright, a Riverdale resident, came to know the Lord, and when he learned of the project I was undertaking, he donated the land to build the tabernacle. Velty and his wife, Lena, would become two of my family's dearest friends.

Finally, in late summer of 1943, the Riverdale open-air tabernacle was completed. We scheduled our first service for 2:00 P.M. on a Sunday afternoon and God sent us the people. They came from several different Protestant denominations, but all with one purpose in mind, to win others. Speakers from the Brethren, Methodist, Baptist, and Nazarene churches took turns presenting the gospel of Jesus Christ. Even with no pastor, we grew in numbers. Before summer had passed, Brothers J. H. Mason, L.R. Higgins, and W.B. Dobbins had spoken. Two other men, Brothers Hillman and Bailey, also spoke. (*I am sorry I can no longer remember their first names*). All of these men were powerful speakers and passionate soul winners for the Lord

Even before the organization of the tabernacle congregation as a local church, we began cottage prayer meetings on Friday evenings. These were incredible times of worship, fellowship and praise. We were invited into homes of Roanoke, Franklin, Bedford and Botetourt

Counties, as well as Roanoke City, Vinton, and Salem. God moved in mighty ways, and I was happy to be a part of the movement.

Weeks passed, and the Lord never let up speaking to me. One beautiful sunny morning, Joyce and I went for a walk. When the poet wrote, *'God's in His heaven, all's right with the world',* he must have been experiencing a day such as we had then. That is how lovely the day was. At that time, however, my world was far from being all right. The war raging in my heart far outweighed the fear I had of the fighting in Europe and the Far East. While Joyce tugged on my arm for me to speed up my stride, God tugged at my heart for me to relinquish control of my life. I knew I was fighting a force far superior to any I had ever encountered. Finally, on this day, when I no longer could stand the pressure, I began to sob. My child looked on as I fell to my knees. "Daddy," Joyce asked, "why are you crying?"

I took that lovely little creature of innocence into my arms and held her close to my heart. As the tears continued to flow, she caught them in the tiny strands of hair falling over her young shoulders. "Daddy's talking to Jesus," I told her. What more could I have said?

Several weeks later, following a Sunday morning service, Mrs. Riggels, a dear old saint more than ninety years of age, shook my hand, and then lingered on to speak with me. "Let me tell you something, young man," she said, "God is calling you to preach, and you had better obey." I wondered how this woman could have possibly known what was going on in my heart. Was my misery that obvious to the world? I truly believe God used Mrs. Riggels to encourage me to do His will.

Cold weather was upon us, and the outdoor tabernacle had no walls. The men in our church assembled to discuss the issue. "We need a pastor," said Mr. Roby McVey, "and I think Brother Robert Painter should have the job."

I could not believe what I heard him say. Here was a man who actually believed I could preach. McVey's proposal not only surprised me, but it also erased my doubts concerning God's calling. If God wanted me, and the people wanted me, then what else could I do, but try.

On my way home from the meeting, I wondered what Ginny would say about having a preacher for a husband. After all, I thought, she knows me better than anyone knows me. As soon as I walked into the house, I told her. "Guess what, Honey? God's called me to preach."

"You can't do that," she responded while looking me right in the eyes. "You don't know how."

"Well, I'll just have to do it anyway," I replied, "because I don't have any choice in the matter. It's what God wants, and the people too. They need a pastor and have asked me to help them."

Ginny looked away from me, and for a moment or two she said nothing. Then she looked at me again. "Robert," she said, "you are not a preacher but, if you insist on doing this, I won't stand in your way." She lowered her eyes, and while staring at the floor, she whispered, "I will not go with you because it simply would be too embarrassing."

I rebelled no longer. "With God's help," I told the men, "I will do my best to be a good pastor."

Ginny, true to her word, did not go with me to church. She was pregnant with our second daughter, Charlotte, so for her, pregnancy was a compelling reason not to go. My wife loved me and wanted God's will for our lives, but she did not relish being a minister's wife. I know she trusted God, but she just could not see him using somebody like me.

A couple of months went by, and then on a beautiful summer morning, Lena Wright called Ginny. "We're having such nice weather," she said, "that Velty and I thought you and Bob might like to share a picnic lunch with us tomorrow. Can you make it?"

"Sounds good to me," Ginny replied. "Where are we going?"

"I believe you will love the place. It's a beautiful park in Rocky Mount, and by the way, you don't need to bring anything because I have enough food for all of us."

We very much enjoyed the company of Velty and Lena, so we were happy for the invitation. Following our Sunday morning worship service, the Wrights and I picked up Ginny at home, and the four of us rode to the park. The women put out a big spread of delicious fried chicken, coleslaw, potato salad, and coconut pie. It was a very nice picnic. After we ate, we chatted about the morning service, and then began clearing the table.

"I was just thinking," Velty said while he placed the picnic basket in the trunk of the car, "the old folks' home is just down the road. Perhaps we should go there and talk with some of the residents. You know how lonesome they must be. Maybe we can cheer them up with some good scriptures verses."

"That's a good idea," I said, shaking my head in approval. "There is plenty of time before the evening service."

After our spouses agreed to visit the shut-ins, the four of us dropped by the nursing home and chatted with a number of its residents.

"Would you like to hear Brother Painter preach?" Velty asked occupants as we moved from one room to the other. Every one of them begged me to stay and speak.

"Okay," I told Velty. "If the girls are not anxious to get home, I'll preach."

Ginny heard me publicly speak for the first time. On the way home, she was quiet. She thought the Wrights planned the picnic for the purpose of the nursing home visit-that she would be forced to hear me preach. I believe my wife was appalled at what she heard, but I believe too, she was a bit proud. That evening, she dressed and went with me to the Sunday night service. From that day forward, she was a part of the ministry, my partner while serving the Lord.

I suppose there is no better time than now to talk about my tears. There are many questions asked as to why I shed so many of them. I actually do not know the answer, but I can tell you that my tears come from God. I learned this through two answered prayers.

At the onset of my ministry, I believed my tears to be an obstacle that I should overcome. My thoughts were that the tears hindered my delivery of the message. I wanted so much for them to go away, but I could not stop crying. One morning when it was time for me to feed my hogs, this burden weighed heavily upon my heart. I thought about it all the way down to the hog pen and decided that I would just ask God to take the tears away. If I could not preach without crying, then why preach at all. The only comfort I could give myself was a reminder that God would answer this prayer just as He had with the cigarettes.

It was early morning just before sunrise, and I suppose I could have found a better place to pray. There is something in nature, however, that brings us closer to the Lord. (*You know, we could prepare sermons from what we learn in nature. A vegetable garden, a fruit-bearing tree, a vine, the birth of a baby farm animal-they all speak to us of the mighty hand of our Creator. I think that is the reason I have always loved farming. Watching a seed grow into a beautiful fruit tree, or seeing vegetables buried beneath the ground ought to draw anybody closer to God. I never tire of watching things grow. Whenever I need to be alone with God, I simply walk into my garden and He is everywhere).* Anyway, that morning while I was feeding the hogs I felt the same way, so after filling the hogs' trough, I knelt on my knees right in the muck. "Lord," I prayed, "you have got to take these tears from me, or I'll never be able to preach." That was all I needed to say; a strange, eerie feeling swept over me and I knew God had answered my prayer.

Several days passed, and I was concerned about the delivery of my sermon on Sunday morning. I did not pray again about the tears because I knew God heard and answered my prayer. The tears were gone. When the time comes, I assured myself, you will do just fine. Now, when I think about it, I should have known I was not in the will of God, because if I honestly thought I was in His will, then why was I so worried?

Finally, it was Sunday, and the time came for me to preach. Even as I walked to the podium and opened my Bible, I was not comfortable. I choked on the first words. For a moment, I could not swallow, and I stammered even with the reading of scripture. How I ever made it through that message, I will never know, but I knew when it ended, where my next stop was to be-the hog pen. When I was finally home, I went into the muck for a second time. "Lord," I cried, "if you want me to be a crying preacher then give me back my tears. I can't preach without them."

Folks, the tears came back, and they never left me again. I cannot tell you the reason for them. I guess they come from a burdened heart. I only know God wants me to have them. Perhaps tears can stir a hardened heart that my stammering tongue could not otherwise reach. I just thank God that His ways are not our ways.

Broken Vessels

Oh, to be clay in the Great Potter's hands
Broken then shaped to His will
A vessel He empties and makes fit for use
A life to be molded and filled

A vessel He's chosen to be like His Son
Transformed by the way of His cross
Washed in the blood that He shed for man's sin
Then sent to a world that is lost

Chapter 07

Laborers Together

Jan.1944–Dec.1949

• •

"For we are labourers together with God;"

By 1944, I had found steady work and Ginny was about to give birth to our second child, one who decided she would make her entrance into the world in such a manner that no one involved could forget. It all began on March 19, 1944 during a vicious snowstorm, or perhaps blizzard would be a better word to describe the weather.

"Bob," Ginny said to me around 10:00 P.M., "You had better get Lena and the doctor. I am about to have this baby."

"Immediately, I called the doctor, took Joyce to her grandmother, and then went to pick up Lena who was to assist the doctor.

"Where is the doctor?" Lena asked as I parked the car in front of our house.

"I don't know. He should be here. I telephoned him before I came to get you."

"I hope he is not stranded somewhere. If he is, you and I are in big trouble."

Inside the house, we found that Ginny's labor was rapidly progressing. Lena scurried around, making preparations for what lay ahead, and I repeatedly looked out the window to see if the doctor was anywhere in sight. There was nothing outside but snow and more snow.

I boiled water and paced the floor while keeping my ears open for the sound of a vehicle. Frankly, I was so scared that I never stopped praying-not even for a moment. Suddenly, I thought I heard tires spinning on Riverdale Hill and eagerly went to investigate. Sure enough, it was the doctor. By this time, it was early morning of March 20. When we were finally able to get home, Lena met us at the door.

"The little girl couldn't wait," she said while grinning from ear to ear. "She's on the bed with her mama."

Charlotte Elizabeth

If the doctor had not been with me, and I had seen that child on the bed, I would have gone into a state of panic. Wrapped in a pink blanket with her umbilical cord still attached, she was a remarkable sight! The bed was in shambles, and Ginny appeared to be in shock. Even while he was taking care of the squalling infant, the doctor attempted to calm my nerves. "What name are you giving the little girl?" he asked.

"Charlotte Elizabeth," I responded while touching Ginny to see if she was still breathing.

"Charlotte Elizabeth," the doctor said after me. I think we have a princess somewhere in England named Elizabeth." He chuckled, paused, and then added, "It sure is a pretty name-most likely be some time, though, before she can put the two together."

Actually, it was more than some time before Charlotte could put her two names together. She jokingly tells people that she was in the third grade before she could write all of it. What a joy this child has been to our lives! She was, and is a lovely and beautiful daughter.

A little irony to this story is that one year before all of this happened Lena had asked Ginny to help with the delivery of her daughter, Carol Anne. Ginny refused by saying, 'I'm afraid the baby might come early, and I wouldn't know what to do'.

Not long after the birth of Charlotte, Ginny and I went house searching. For a number of years, we had been living in four rooms, and with a growing family, we needed to think about a larger place, one of our own. Aside from that, whenever we hosted a cottage prayer meeting, people packed into the rental house like sardines in a can. One day, I found what I thought to be the perfect place for us. There was land enough for a garden, chickens, and a couple of hogs.

I loved the place, but an unmarried man occupied it for several years and it needed many repairs. When Ginny saw it, she cried. The walls of the house were dirty from a coal-burning heater, and the yard was a disaster. Finally, after promising her I would make it a beautiful place, my wife agreed for us to purchase the Mississippi Avenue property. Everything that I promised her I would do to the house, I did, and

Mississippi Avenue Home

more; I even built her a white picket fence around the yard. Ginny must have learned to like the house quite a bit because it stayed our home for the next 35 years.

In January of 1945, I had been a Christian for 3 years. Two months from this anniversary, I was officially ordained as a minister of the Lord Jesus Christ. That day, I will never forget. Rev. John T. Kenyon from Asheboro, NC and Rev. L.R. Higgins of Roanoke ministered the charge. On the church committee were Orey Lee, John Hutchens, Roby McVey, Velty Wright, and Moody Thurman.

On April 30, 1945, Adolf Hitler committed suicide, and on May 8, Germany surrendered to the Allied Forces; the war in Europe ended. Following the Potsdam Declaration by the Allies, in August of 1945, the United States dropped atomic bombs on Hiroshima and Nagasaki, and with this destruction and loss of life, the Japanese also surrendered. Finally, with the killing and devastations of World War II halted, American G.I.s returned home to a fabulous celebration of victory, and our country began to help the war-torn nations of Europe and Asia rebuild. The horror of those two bombings of Japan, however, stunned the whole world, and ever since the day we dropped them, they have been a topic for discussion.

A grateful America did not forget all that happened in those war-torn years. Most of our country's families attended church every Sunday, even those that had not suffered the loss of a loved one. At the tabernacle, our Riverdale church family increased in numbers and God gave us the building we so vitally needed. From several denominations, Christians came to work with us; all were united in the Lord. We continued holding services at the tabernacle and at many locations throughout the Roanoke Valley. Cottage prayer meetings continued to be a real blessing to those who attended them, and as a result, many souls found Jesus as their personal Savior.

In 1946, I was a full-time minister, but I also worked for the railroad. One day, I had a terrible burning in my nostrils that worsened as the day progressed. The company sent me to see Dr. H. B. Jones who told me my tonsils were infected and that the infection had spread. I was to go home, not preach and get bed rest for two weeks. I was then to have my tonsils removed. I decided that if I was not going to work for two weeks then I should go and see Ma and Pa before the surgery. Still ill, I went for a visit to Montebello.

While I was visiting with my folks, a Pentecostal minister came by and asked me if I would come and preach a revival for him. "I'll take my old pick-up," he said, "and go door to door so people will know we're having the meetings."

I agreed to do this for the minister, knowing that I probably should be in bed as the doctor instructed, but one of my problems is being able to say no if somebody asks me to preach.

My mom and dad were not yet Christians, so I prayed they would come to the meetings. Neither of them was hesitant to do so. I thank God that I made the decision to hold those meetings because on one of those nights, He gave me the honor of leading my mother to the foot of the cross.

Pa did not heed the calling for many years to come. Actually, it was probably in the mid- 1950s when I asked Brother Cecil Wimmer one day to go with me to talk to my dad about his salvation. Pa had a heart problem, and I was afraid that he might go out of this world without knowing the Lord. Cecil and I prayed that God would cause Pa's heart to be receptive to His Word, and He truly did answer our prayers. On that visit, my dad accepted Jesus Christ as his own personal Savior. By the way, he lived for a number of years after his salvation.

Before the ending of 1945, as always when things are happening for the Lord, unrest began to build within the tabernacle's church body. Some members of the congregation were not happy because we were not associated with a mainstream denomination. After much prayer and discussion, the men of the church began to consider those denominations whose doctrines aligned with the majority of our beliefs. One of the Nazarene men told me that his denomination would like the church to be a part of their organization, and so I contacted its district director, a brother whose family name was Keyes. Brother Keyes and the Nazarenes were more than glad to have us join them, and so we agreed to a merger with a trial period of two years. Just two months following the end of those two years, 1 was no longer the Riverdale tabernacle's pastor. At the Nazarene's 1947 Annual State Meeting, the conference had elected a new Regional Director. He decided that my lack of education should prevent me from pastoring a church, and that a college graduate should replace me.

My work at the tabernacle was finished, but it had not been in vain. Various denominations established new churches in the area, and a couple of them even built their sanctuaries on the same property where we held our tent meetings. Recognizing this, Nazarene officials offered me a position as a helper in planting churches. I knew this was not what God called me to do, so I declined their offer. Since I did not receive a salary from the church, it was necessary for me to work a full time secular job to support my family, and I could not have done so with the Nazarenes' offer. I simply told the officials that I would follow God's leading.

Expelled from the same church I had worked so hard to found was one big disappointment. When it happened, there was a lot of emotional turmoil for me, but I purposed in my heart not to be angry. To do so would have been without faith. God, I knew was on His throne, and my future was in His hands. On the Sunday we said 'good-bye' to our friends in Riverdale, children and adults alike were in tears. No one understood why this separation had to be.

While I was still pastoring the tabernacle, I also conducted services in a little mission located in the southeast section of Roanoke. Pastor Reynolds of Stove Creek Baptist Church had opened the mission on Wise Avenue and asked for my help. It was there, at this mission, I met Brother Bob Mays. Bob's salvation came to him through the ministry of a little 12 year-old girl, Renee Morris, who held a citywide revival in Roanoke. Following his conversion, he came to the mission in search of a church home. This man grew steadily in the Lord and became a champion in the work of the Lord Jesus Christ. He and his wife, Florence were my lifelong friends and confidants. Members of their family became workers at the House of Prayer, and two of their girls, Jean Porter and Betty Wiseman, are still with the church.

In those days, Brother Bob was with me wherever I went. Even before I left Riverdale, he and his little girl, Shirley, faithfully attended our services.

One day Bob approached me with good news. "There's an old Apostolic Church," he said, "over on 17th Street. It does not have but one room, but no one is using it, and it would be a perfect place to hold Sunday afternoon services."

For a little while, we discussed the possibility of this happening. Brother Bob was persistent. "The lady who owns it is a Mrs. Creasy," he said, "and I am almost sure we can rent it. Pray about it, and if God wants you to preach there, He'll make it happen."

I really felt that God was leading me into this endeavor. We contacted Mrs. Creasy and rented the property. After much cleaning and fixing-up, the doors opened on Sunday afternoon, August 3, 1947. Thirty-eight people joined us for the service. The following Sunday, the number rose to 60. I was comfortable knowing we were in the will of God.

Immediately, we saw souls saved and believers growing into a church body. Having experienced such excellent relationships with Christians whose doctrinal beliefs sometimes differed, I never once considered becoming entangled again with church boards governed by a mainstream denomination. My people understood this viewpoint and agreed with me. Matthew 21:13 and Mark 11:17 tells us *"My house shall be called the house of prayer."* From these verses came the name for our new church, "The House of Prayer" in Roanoke, Virginia. Our motto became and is today…

> *"No membership but fellowship;*
> *No creed but Christ;*
> *No book but the Bible"*

At the House of Prayer, we began the same basic ministries as we had in Riverdale, and this included cottage prayer meetings. The most memorable of these meetings was one we held early in the 17th Street ministry. Joseph M. Beckner, Sr. and his wife, Gussie, lived on Wise Avenue in Southeast Roanoke, and our prayer meeting was taking place in the home of their next-door neighbor. Attending the service, were Joe, Sr.'s family members, Joe, Jr. *(better known as Jack)*, and the elder Joe's son-in-law, Benjamin Fulton. Not one of these men was a Christian.

The prayer group, consisting of my people and folks who lived in the neighborhood, was well into the meeting when a ruckus at the front door interrupted it. After drinking too much alcohol, the senior Beckner returned home. He was so intoxicated that he entered the wrong house *(both houses were built exactly alike)* and found himself in a prayer meeting. God must have been somewhere at work in the midst of this because before the prayer meeting ended, all three men in this family were wondrously saved. For many years, Jack and Ben worked with us in the field of evangelism and eventually, Ben was ordained into the ministry. The elder Beckner became active in the church, as well as a trustee for the House of Prayer. When the church finally purchased its own building, he put his home up for collateral. For all of the remaining years of their lives, the Beckner family was dedicated to the work of the Lord. Ben and Josephine Fulton's daughter, Darla, was the first child I dedicated to the Lord, and Gussie was one of the best Sunday school teachers the House of Prayer children ever had. Joe Beckner passed away March 12, 1981. As of this writing Jack and his family are serving the Lord in Roanoke with New Life Christian Ministries, and little Darla Fulton grew up to become Mrs. John Allman, Jr.. God does some remarkable things!

When we held our first service at the House of Prayer, we had no piano. Knowing we could use a mobile instrument in all of our ministries, we purchased a portable organ. I told my daughter she was going to play for us. She was learning to play the piano, and could play a couple of hymns. Now, Joyce was just a youngster whose feet would not even reach the pedals of the organ, but not to be outdone, she sat in the lap of an adult who pumped the organ for her. While the child repeatedly played the same two hymns, we sang to her music.

God always supplied us with outstanding musicians. A few weeks after we began the work, he sent to us Mrs. Elizabeth Amos. She was an excellent pianist, and believing she would be with us indefinitely, the church purchased a piano. Mrs. Amos, however, lived some distance from the church, so she was with us less than a year. Mildred Hutchinson, one of our teen-agers, was taking piano lessons at the Baptist Goodwill Center, and as young as she was, Mildred readily stepped in and became our new pianist. Wherever the services took us-street meetings, cottage prayer meetings, or tent revivals, Mildred was there. Sometimes, she played the piano while Joyce plugged away at the organ, and sometimes, it was the other way around. The two girls complemented one another. I have many fond memories of Mildred's talents, both as pianist and singer. Mostly, I remember her faithfulness. We missed her when she married and moved to Richmond.

Another musician came to us from Rock, WV. She was not one of our regulars, but was indeed, a blessing to all who attended our revival services. Miss Edna Ratliff's talent was outstanding, and she loved the Lord with all of her heart. She played her accordion with much fervor, and those who heard her sing, will not forget her good southern gospel singing. The song most requested was *"Something Got a Hold of Me"*. Often, while singing, Edna would feel the spirit, stop singing, and share a personal testimony. Those testimonies stirred the hearts of believers and drew people into our services. Today, she is Edna Holshouser and remains to be a dear friend.

At the onset of House of Prayer ministries, Mr. Howard Mitchell and Miss Melva Webb also contributed to our church music program. Howard directed our singing and Melva was a soloist. She could sing *"Under His Wings"* like no other singer I have heard. Melva was not with us long; leaving for full-time Christian service, she went to the mission field of Brazil.

The House of Prayer grew quickly, just as quickly as the Riverdale tabernacle. God gave us many talented leaders-teachers, speakers, musicians, and other workers. Mr. W.B. Dobbins was our first Sunday School Superintendent and also serving in this capacity were men such as Steve Porter, Ben Fulton, and Cecil Wimmer. Bob Mays, Ellis Turner, Joe Beckner, Velty Wright, and Cecil Wimmer handled church business, and our first Sunday school teachers were Mr. Velty Wright, Mrs. Florence Mays, Miss Ada Mae McNeil, Mrs. Joe Beckner, Mr. and Mrs. Gordon Camden, Mrs. Doris Vest, and others. I believe Mrs. Dorothy Hutchinson and her girls were the church's first custodians. These are but a few of the workers who contributed to the beginning of this new work. I always hate to name folks because I would never want to leave someone out, but those whose names I can recall and who were there at the very beginning, I cannot refrain from mentioning.

They say there is a story to every life and all of the workers named above most likely have something remarkable they could tell about God's work in their lives. All of their stories I do not know, but many I am familiar with. The conversion of Cecil Wimmer is one such story. Cecil lived around the corner from the House of Prayer and had family members who came to the church. This man wanted no part of God. He was living a life much the way my life was before I met the Lord. One day, I went to see Cecil, and stood on the sidewalk of his home. "You need to give your life to God," I told him. "Why don't you just come to one of my services?"

I did not know if Cecil was listening or not, but the following Sunday, he and his son, Buddy came to hear me preach. Viola, Cecil's wife, was a Seventh Day Adventist and was reluctant to join him, but Cecil continued to come, and eventually, Viola came too. I believe it was during one of our revivals that God gloriously saved both of them.

A couple of years later, Cecil and Viola went through a terrible time of grief and sorrow. One morning, their infant son, Leon, began to run an extremely high fever. Immediately, he was taken to a hospital where he was diagnosed with spinal meningitis. In a matter of hours, little Leon was in heaven. If Cecil and Viola had not known the Lord,

I do not know if they could have made it through that tragedy. While she clung to the arm of her husband, Cecil led his broken-hearted wife from the graveside. As she turned and looked back, someone heard her say, 'Mama will meet you in heaven.' I do not believe either mother or father ever fully recovered from that loss.

Cecil became one of our most faithful workers and supporter of the House of Prayer's ministries. *(I will tell you later how God answered prayer for Cecil in miraculous ways).* A number of years later, Cecil, Jr. (Buddy), the oldest son in the Wimmer family, became husband to our daughter, *(the one with the long name, Charlotte Elizabeth Painter. When that happened, she had to add "Wimmer" to all of that spelling).*

During our two plus years on 17th Street, God blessed us in more ways than I can say. Continuously, we saw souls saved, and revivals with preachers like Brother J. H. Mason brought much spiritual growth to new converts. We had one well-remembered series of meetings with a group of 18 young men from God's Bible School in Cincinnati, Ohio. The boys, known as G.I.s of the Cross were undoubtedly Spirit-filled believers. While they were with us, they slept in tents near Brother Bob Mays' home. During the daytime, the students rode in military jeeps up and down Roanoke City streets using megaphones to invite people to our meetings. Their gospel messages saturated the hearts of those who responded to the invitations. The boys' sermons convicted hearts, and the music was outstanding. Those services turned into quite a revival with numerous souls saved.

When 1948 dawned upon us, Ginny and I were also about to be revived, and it was not going to be a spiritual matter. Soon, we would welcome the fourth female into our home.

This birth did not take place during a snowstorm, but it easily could have been for it happened on February 23, 1948. Because we had so much to praise our God for, we decided to call the little bundle of joy Gloria Jean. Still the only male in our household,

Gloria Jean

I was beginning to feel outnumbered, but oh, how I loved my girls-all of them! God continued to bless us. Gloria came to us well and healthy, and we were thankful, ever so thankful! They say God gives men girls to teach us tenderness so if this is true, then God must have thought me to be a very tough person, and I suppose I was. Just the same, He was surely blessing me, and not only with a growing family, but with a growing church!

The summer of 1948 was busy, busy, busy, and then in a blaze of glory, autumn came to the Roanoke Valley. Red, gold, brown and orange leaves filled our parks, farmlands, and city streets. On 17th Street, the House of Prayer went from one season into the other. Sunday morning and evening services, tent revivals, child evangelism classes, and weekly cottage prayer meetings were the norm, but there were also street meetings on the market square in Roanoke as well as other parts of the city. Our church family also participated in the ministries of the Roanoke City Rescue Mission.

Nothing we do in life is 100% without problems, and accidents are going to happen. In the fall of 1948, my old Plymouth was about to see its last days. I had driven it thousands of miles. Ginny and I decided instead of purchasing another used vehicle, we would step out on faith and buy a new one, and so I went to a Ford dealership where the new 1949 Fords had just arrived. They were beautiful! After deciding we could afford the purchase, we drove home a bright and shiny black 4-door sedan. Most of you have been there, so I do not need to tell you how happy we were with that first new car.

The '49 Ford was one of the manufacturer's most popular vehicles. Young people loved it. At the time of our car purchase, the church was holding tent meetings in Hardy near Woodrow Morgan's home, and when I arrived there with a new car, all of the kids gathered around it.

"Can we look at the inside, Preacher Painter? Can we?"

The kids were as excited as I was. Unable to resist their pleadings, I stepped aside so they could all look.

"Can we see the trunk too?" one of the boys asked.

I went to the trunk and pulled on the handle. The lid came up and five or six heads were soon inside. After all of their o-o s and ahs, the kids stepped backwards, and I slammed the lid. One piercing scream

shattered the airwaves. Little Diane Turner, preschooler of Brother Ellis and Sister Winnie Turner, stood there with her head bleeding profusely. The child continued to scream and cry. I did not know anything to do but pray. I grabbed Diane's little head between my hands, and with her body close to mine, I desperately prayed! Immediately, the bleeding stopped. Those who witnessed that incident say God healed her. I do not know if that was a miraculous healing, or not. I do know something happened because we never heard of any sustainable injury. Without ever seeing a doctor, amazingly, the child's head healed. I have never forgotten her, and still cannot help but wonder if God did touch her head while I prayed.

The car accident was not the only problem I encountered while having services in Hardy. One evening during a cottage prayer meeting, I became feverish and congested. I simply did not feel well at all. I continued with the service because I did not wish to disappoint those in attendance, and I have never been one to run to the doctor with every little sniffle.

"Your cough is terrible, Brother Painter. You should see a doctor because I believe you are more ill than you realize." Velty sounded as if he was terribly concerned about my condition. "I can take you to the emergency room at Lewis Gale."

The Lewis Gale Hospital was in Roanoke, so Velty, after convincing me that I should go, went with me. When the doctor listened to my heart and lungs, my cough was deep and continuous.

"You either have a bad flu bug or pneumonia," he said. "We're going to put you in a room for a few days."

"No, no, Doc, you can't do that. I have to preach on Sunday."

The doctor smiled and shook his head. "Then, we'll just have to preach in the hospital, won't we? There's no way you're leaving here before Monday."

I was shocked and disappointed but true to his word, the doctor kept me confined there for several days. God has His way of slowing us down.

Back at the House of Prayer sanctuary, there was another problem, a GOOD problem known as growing pains. We were outgrowing the building. Not only did we need more seating capacity and Sunday

school classes, we needed bathrooms. There was not a single toilet in the building, and nowhere to put one. The place simply was not large enough for a growing congregation.

Our God, however, knew all about this problem, and unbeknown to us, He was providing. A genuine church building, located only two blocks from 17th street, was waiting for us to call it the House of Prayer. A group of people in fellowship with the Church of God owned the church and had it up for auction. The building was much larger than the one we were in, and I was certain God wanted us to have it. I had no idea how we could make a purchase such as this because those leaner years of the Great Depression had taken their toll on people's finances. My church people were not wealthy by any means, so I knew there was no money for a down payment. Nevertheless, on November 11, 1949, I took a day off from work at the gas company and went to the auction. Another man who undoubtedly wanted the property was also there. When the bid reached $4,000, he and I were the only two offering bids.

"I will give you $4200," the second bidder said.

"Forty-four," I bid.

"Forty-five," I then heard.

I better not bid over $5,000, I said to myself, and then made a bid of $4,700.

"Well," said the second man. "I came here with $4,500 in mind, so this is where I stop bidding.

With the bid of $4,700, I received the contract. One question remained…how was the church going to pay for it?

I left the auction, and drove to the Colonial American Bank and asked to speak with its president.

"How may I help you, young man?"

I did not want the man to see me grinning, so I put my hand over my mouth, and pulled the contract from my coat pocket.

"This is a contract," I said. "I am the pastor of the House of Prayer, and I just made a bid of $4,700 on this church property. Is it possible for the church to get a mortgage with you?"

The president sat down at a desk and asked me to have a seat on the other side.

"What kind of collateral does the church have?" he asked.

I shook my head back and forth. "None," I said to him.

"Are you saying your church has no money?"

"We have absolutely nothing."

"Well then, what about your members? Surely, you have men in the church with collateral."

"Like what?"

"Stock, bonds, real estate, even homes. Sometimes church members allow their homes to stand for collateral. Telephone a couple of your men and ask for their help. I guarantee you that they will come up with something of value."

I made phone calls to Brothers Cecil Wimmer, Joe Beckner, and Ellis Turner. They joined me at the bank, and with the help of the president, we worked out a deal. The four of us used our homes as collateral. Thirty-five dollars a month was all the church needed to cover the mortgage. Again, I saw what God does when we step out on faith. I had bid on that building not knowing if the church could even meet a monthly mortgage payment.

When the men went to see what we purchased, we found the entrance boarded up. If we were going to have Sunday school rooms, the basement would have to be hand dug, and definitely, we would need to install bathrooms. The work ahead was monumental, and for a moment, I wondered how in this world we could get it all done. I then remembered the tabernacle in Riverdale. We began there with nothing. On Kirk Avenue, we did have a beginning, a building that would one day belong to the church. Actually, a building that already belonged to God.

The First Children of the House of Prayer.

The House of Prayer's First Revival
Howard Mitchell-Director of Music
Brother Painter-Pastor, H.O. Mason-Evangelist
Edna Ratliff, Mildred Hutchinson-Musicians

· ·

"...there shall be showers of blessings"

Immediately following the purchase of our Kirk Avenue building, we began the renovations. When shovels and picks arrived on the site, the boards on the front of the building came off, and we went to work. While the men of the House of Prayer dug out mounds of red clay beneath the foundation, days passed into weeks, and weeks into months. Finally, construction on the basement was finished. You cannot imagine how delightful it was to see those classrooms and restrooms where that clay had once been. When the renovations were completed, our people were ready for revival. The church family tithed its money the way it should tithe, and within six short years, we were burning the final note on the mortgage. On the day we burned that note, we also dedicated a new organ. Joyce was glad to see that.

During the 1950s, we conducted tent meetings regularly, and God blessed the House of Prayer abundantly. We had no less than three revivals a year, and no less than two prayer meetings a week. Often, a single revival would last for a month. In the summer of 1950, one tent meeting held at Moneta in Bedford County lasted three months. So many people responded to the gospel that no one bothered to record the number of conversions. That summer, I preached 88 nights in tent meetings besides our regular church services. My *"cup runneth over"!*

Meantime, the United States was again at war, sacrificing American lives for the cause of freedom. This time, we were in Korea. As Americans always do in wartime, we began to turn even more to the God of our fathers. Most of us were still apprehensive about the losses of World War II, and remembering the "A" bomb, we did not know what to expect next. At this moment in history, Mao Tse Tung of China was murdering scores of people, Stalin put millions of Russians to death, and now Korea was killing its own-all for the same ideology-Communism. World War II ended with Germany divided, and the remaining countries of Europe lived in fear of Russia pouncing on them. We never knew who would be the next victims of this movement devouring the other side of the world. *(It appears to me that man's lust for power takes us from one tyrant to another, usually the next one more evil that the one before. I suppose we have seen nothing as to what it will be when that final tyrant arrives on the scene. This world is certainly ripe for the anti-Christ, isn't it?).*

As we watched the Korean War escalate, we watched the first children of the House of Prayer grow up. I believe our pianist, Mildred Hutchinson, was the first to graduate from high school, and then in 1954, she was married to Roger St. Clair. The two met in Blue Ridge while

Mildred was playing the piano for our tent revival. Her sister, Betty (*my co-author*) in the same year, married Roger's cousin, Everett *(Pete)* Jones. He was also from Blue Ridge and attended the tent meetings. In 1955, Shirley Mays *(the same who came with her daddy to the Riverdale Tabernacle)* married Lee Jones. Thereafter, the HP kids married so quickly until I do not remember whom, or when, they wed. In 1955, I did not have a license to marry couples, but within the next year, I acquired one. On January 5, 1957, I married William Hurt and Pauline Dobbins, and in 1958, Edmund Robtison and Iris Thurman married. Those two marriages were the House of Prayer's first weddings.

Some of these weddings took place during the Korean conflict and others after the ending of it. I say conflict because that is what we called the Korean War. The Asian country is divided today, half of it, a democracy and the other half, communism. One of these days, we will see them fighting again.

The House of Prayer church family was increasing in numbers because one family brought in another. In those days, there were still some large families, often with six or eight children. This created an atmosphere where folks felt welcomed, especially new converts. The tent meetings continued for eight years, and as we continued to win souls; if they came to our church, they brought others with them. Other churches, too, benefited from the tent meetings because all new converts did not always come to the House of Prayer. Keep in mind we held those meetings in several counties.

People who attended the House of Prayer and lived outside our immediate area needed transportation, so to *"bring them in"* we began a bus ministry. Brother Bill Grant headed up this ministry. The bus route began from Bill's home in Salem, and then went to Glenvar to pick up four or five families there. Other families who lived in a northwest Roanoke housing development also rode on his bus.

When you think about it, we were actually a Roanoke Valley congregation because there were people from various localities worshipping with us. Some families drove a number of miles to the House of Prayer. Families such as the Wrights, the Mays family, the Thurmans, and the Conners came from the Garden City area of Roanoke where we had conducted several open-air meetings. The cottage prayer meetings in Franklin County brought us the Hurts and the Morgans. Families, such as the Leonards, Womacks, and Cadds traveled from Botetourt County. Our 1951 tent revival in Blue Ridge brought these families to us. People, saved as the result of street meetings and those who found the Lord through the rescue mission, sometimes found their way to the House of Prayer. Many others traveled a number of miles to worship with us, but I cannot remember all of them. In order to fulfill the Great Commission in Roanoke City, the House of Prayer reached out to the lost, the downtrodden, the grief-stricken, and the sick. The Bible tells us to *"compel them to come in",* and so we did!

Here is a rather humorous story old-timers like to tell about one of our street meetings. Across the street from where we conducted services on Roanoke's Jamison Avenue, there was a *"beer joint".* Its customers often came outside for our meetings. One Sunday afternoon, there was a woman in the group. When I began to preach, I noticed several people leaning against the walls of the building, but I honestly did not notice anything unusual about any of them. During my sermon, I said something I wanted to emphasize, so I made this statement, *'If the shoe fits you, wear it'.* Now, all of us have heard that cliché, but apparently, the woman across the way had not. I did not see her slip the shoe from her foot, but she thought I had, and took the remark personally. Furiously, she marched across the street, gave me a mean look, and then bellowed, "I want you to know that I took my shoe off because I have a corn on my toe and it's about to kill me."

I found it very difficult to hold back the chuckles, but somehow I managed to do so. I apologized by telling the woman that I did not know her shoe was off. I think the incident probably would not have happened had she been sober, but it was a rather humorous happening. Whatever happened to the woman, I cannot say, but it would be good to know that she found the Lord.

One of the biggest happenings of the fifties was the founding of House of Prayer in Floyd County. In 1952, Marlin Guilliams was saved in one of our cottage prayer meetings.

"Will you hold another prayer meeting for us in Floyd?" asked Marlin. "We can hold it at Alvie Guilliams' house."

I agreed to this, and a number of people showed up for our meeting. While we were there, those in attendance asked if I would speak on Saturday nights at Silver Leaf Church of the Brethren. After much soul searching and prayer, I again honored their request. We held a revival at Silver Leaf in December of that year, and several local residents, Raymond Peters, Mamie Radford, Kaufman, Clyde, and J.C. Thompson gave their hearts to the Lord. The converts continued to worship at Silver Leaf, but as they grew in the faith, they realized there were irreconcilable differences in their beliefs. The new Christians prayed, asking God to guide them.

Finally, the group began organizing a new church, the second House of Prayer. When the founders asked me to be their pastor, Sundays were firmly and fully committed to the Roanoke House of Prayer, however, I wanted to accommodate these new believers, so I agreed to switch the Saturday night services at Silver Leaf to this new assembly. A Floyd County family donated land for a building, and on September 6, 1953, the doors of their new building opened, and I found myself pastoring two bodies of believers.

The Lord truly moved in the Floyd ministry. A spirit of revival broke out, cottage prayer meetings began, and during the warmer months, we held tent revivals. On one occasion, we had a tent revival that lasted for 6 weeks. In fact, so much was happening spiritually in the area until those people who did not like their Saturday nights conflicting with church meetings called me the *"OLD PAINT BUCKET"*.

At about this time in Floyd, John Ingram, an unsaved Sunday school member, gave his heart to the Lord. Later, God called him into the ministry. For a number of years, John was my Assistant Pastor in Floyd, but on December 1, 1982, I resigned, and Brother Ingram became the church's full-time pastor. Today, he is still there. John has been a real asset to me in many ways. Actually, in recent days, John has been a pastor to me. He has also travelled with me to Egypt many times.

Many Roanoke House of Prayer members came to Floyd for Saturday night services, and many attended our revivals. On Saturday evenings, Brother Edgar Poff was my friend and chauffeur.

"I will drive for you," Ed told me one Saturday night. "You have to preach again tomorrow, and I don't want you to be worn out."

With few exceptions, Ed was by my side. He always drove home from the service so I could sleep and be refreshed for the Roanoke services on Sunday. God blessed our work in Floyd just as He continued to do in Roanoke. I consider the work there to be a satellite ministry of the Roanoke House of Prayer. God has done wondrous things through His people who serve there, and I praise His name for those blessings!

Even though we see souls saved, and the work of God progressing, we are never without testing and conflicts. That is how God increases our faith. On one occasion in 1955, I found this to be quite true. At that time, I was teaching a Sunday school class at the Roanoke House of Prayer, and we decided to have a picnic at Crabtree Falls in Nelson County. The trip to the falls was fantastic, as was the picnic, but then our time of testing began, and the day became ever so eventful!

"Daddy," Charlotte screamed to me. "Martha is on that steep slope, and she can't stop. Catch her before she falls."

I looked ahead of me and saw what was happening. Martha Radford was running down a steep mountain trail, and she appeared to be falling face forward. I ran after her, but I did not know how I would ever get to her. I think the Lord must have put wings on my legs because she was far ahead of me, and yet I was able to get to her and slow her down.

Martha's heart was pounding profusely. "I could not stop," she panted. "I don't know why, but I could not even slow myself down!"

I was extremely thankful the young woman did not fall, but on that day, there was trouble, more trouble, and even more trouble. Hilda Thompson, another class member, did become a victim of falling. God was with her too. She only received a few scratches and bruises.

After the group left Crabtree Falls, we went for a visit to my home place. Late in the day, tired and dirty, we all climbed into my car and began the drive down a narrow Irish Creek road. It had rained the night before so the shoulders of the road were very soft. Suddenly, we met a car coming from the opposite direction. I moved over, probably giving the man more road than I should have. Over, and over, tumbled our car-right into the creek!

Charlotte quickly climbed from the vehicle, slamming the door behind her. It jammed so tightly that none of us inside could open it. Neither could my daughter open it from her side. All of us trapped within the vehicle had to escape through windows. There we were with the car upside down in the creek, and not even a telephone nearby. I took off on foot and walked for five or six miles until I found one. It was after dark when I finally contacted Brother Cecil Wimmer. He and Brother Thurman came to our rescue. God was with us that day because we could have been badly injured, or even killed.

Joyce Painter, Myra Hurt, and Pauline and
William Hurt help with the radio ministry

Midway through the 1950s, I felt the Lord was leading me to begin a radio ministry. We followed His direction and what a blessing this ministry has been! I have no way of knowing the number of people who have heard me via radio in the past fifty years, but the program continues even to this day. We began broadcasting from Christiansburg early in 1957, but shortly thereafter, we moved to WRIS in Roanoke. In 1961, we switched to station WKBA. Today, we are still broadcasting from there. Praise God from whom all blessings flow!

In 1960, the House of Prayer did not have a ministry to meet the physical needs of the poor who lived in our community, so we decided to do something to help them. As always, God supplied everything we needed for this undertaking. The Campbell house, located right next door to the church, came up for sale. It was a perfect place for our Helping Hands ministry. We purchased the house and members of the church stocked it with food, clothing, and household items that we thought would benefit those in need. Women of the church donated time there to keep it open several days a week. This missionary endeavor was a real blessing to Roanoke area citizens, especially to those who lived near the church.

Now, you know the devil always tries to hinder a new ministry, and our Helping Hands was no exception. Even before we opened our doors, he was at work. When we purchased the Campbell House, it needed repairs, and as always, I was right there in the middle of taking care of the work. We needed to do some plastering, and I decided to undertake the job without any help. Somehow, during the repairs, the lime I was using found its way into my eyes. Without a phone in the house or in the church, I treated my eyes with a water hose. Later in the day, Charlotte and Buddy came by to see how the work was progressing. By then, my eyes were red and swollen. They were also causing me pain. Charlotte was concerned.

"I will be okay," I told her. "Before you came, I flushed them with water." After the couple went home, I resumed the work. As time passed, the pain worsened.

When the plastering job was finished, I went home with my eyes still burning. Finally, after bathing and dressing, I drove to Gill Memorial Hospital. There, I received treatment for edema, and a lecture from the doctor about taking care of my eyes. We should have had a church phone, but that did not happen until 1962. I suppose we put off installing one because no one was at the church in the daytime.

The same year we had a phone installed, I was 49 years old and about as busy as anyone can be. One day, I came across a piece of property; actually, it was a mountain farm. When I say a mountain, I mean a mountain. I fell in love with it. I saw it as a place where I could relax and enjoy nature, as I knew nature to be when I was growing up. Hunting on the property, I was sure, would be great. I wanted the place, but simply could not decide if I should purchase it or not. The price on it was reasonable, but I was not sure my use would justify the investment. All of my girls were still at home, but Charlotte was to be married later in the year, and soon Gloria would be out of high school. Joyce, not yet married, was also living at home. Perhaps, I thought, she would help me with this.

Knowing Joyce had an excellent job, I presumed we could be partners in the endeavor, but I still gave much prayer and consideration to the idea before asking her. My daughter instantly agreed to the purchase of the property.

There was an old farmhouse on the mountain that I thought we should destroy, but Joyce wanted to salvage it, and so we went to work with a pile of rocks and a jack. I pumped the jack and Joyce did the rock sliding. "I think we need to tear this place down and start over," I repeatedly said to my daughter.

"Anyone can build a new house," Joyce replied, "but we are going to save this one."

After endless hours of work, we finally finished the rock foundation and moved on to other renovations. For thirty years, the old cabin served us well for weekends and hunting retreats. As years passed us by, Joyce finally admitted, "we should have built a new one." Fathers do know best, don't they?

The old cabin we saved for retreats is no longer standing. We replaced it for two permanent homes. Side by side, we enjoy one another's company-Ginny and me, and Joyce and her husband, Don. God knew what He was doing when He put us here on top of the world. He gave us a place where the younger couple is nearby to help us in these aging years of life. It is a place where my three girls can bring their families and get away from the hum-drum of everyday living, and it is also a place to wake up to the sounds of God's creatures in the morning and go to sleep with them at night. Here, where we tend to our vegetables and pull weeds from our flowerbeds, we are constantly working our hands and feet. For some unknown reason, they will not stay still.

Lessons from My Garden

Within my garden bed of flowers
God teaches me so many things
I listen for His gentle voice
And treasure every thought He brings

As covered hands dip into soil
Still moist from rains the night before
There comes to mind the wealth that lies
Upon the earth's most hidden floors

Creepy crawling critters there
I see as struggling lives of men
Who wander aimlessly through life
Imprisoned by the walls of sin

The dandelions and weeds I pull
I think we entertain each day
Misdeeds that grieve the Spirit's work
And take the joys of life away

And when I step upon sharp stones
That cause my limbs beneath me fold
I'm so reminded then of things
That bring us down when not controlled

But, when I look above the earth
I see my Father's wondrous grace
With colored ink, He pens a poem
Upon each flower's lovely face

"He hath made everything beautiful in his time: also he hath
set the world in their heart, so that no man can find out the
work that God maketh from the beginning to the end."

Ecclesiastes 3:11

Chapter 09

Where Jesus Walked

1967

. . . .

"I walked today where Jesus walked, and I felt His presence there."

The prosperity that came to America in the fifties brought with it the beginning of moral decline in the sixties. In the fifties, people remembered what God had done for the nation during World War II, and Korea, but in 1962, prayer was removed from our schools, television began to bring us Hollywood's worst productions, and Elvis Presley filled the airwaves with the sensuous sounds of Rock 'n Roll. By 1964, we had witnessed the assassination of John F. Kennedy, civil rights uprisings, and a substantial increase in crime. Our nation prospered, but prosperity breeds pride, and *"pride goeth before a fall"*. America's spiritual decline was inevitable. Our mothers went into the workforce, our children went away to colleges, and our homes began falling apart.

Whenever we see a decline in society, God's church is not far behind. I saw the beginning of apostasy when "worldliness" crept into The Church *(The Church, as used here, is the universal body of Christian believers)*. Sinners' hearts became hardened, and Christians became discouraged. Discouragement breeds unfaithfulness; making the efforts of church workers less profitable. The gospel that once drew millions to our churches fell on ears that did not hear. What were the ministers of the gospel to do? We find the answer across a broad spectrum of

American missionaries who were once church pastors. They left the pulpits of America to preach the gospel on foreign soils.

I never dreamed God could use me as a missionary in a foreign country, but I knew there was a longing within my heart to see the salvation of souls. To a degree, souls were still being saved in America, but they were few, and far between. I longed for the days of the forties and fifties when people packed out the tent, and revival was real revival, not a series of meetings.

In 1967, Mrs. Dorothy Hutchinson, told some of the House of Prayer supporters about a tour that her daughter, Betty, was taking to the Holy Land. "I sure wish Brother Painter could go on that trip," Dorothy said to her sister, Florence. "I don't know anyone who would appreciate it more."

Florence, wife of Brother Bob Mays, agreed. "We never have done anything like that for him," she responded. "Just think what that would mean to him!"

Like any other Christian, I had always dreamed of this, but I never saw the possibility of it happening. However, the Lord knew what his plans were for my future, and every detail that was necessary for me to take that tour fell into place.

The three-week Middle East tour, guided by Rev. Arthur Taylor of Grand Rapids, Michigan originated from New York City in March of 1967. On the itinerary were tours with flights out of Athens, Cairo, Beirut, Damascus, Jerusalem, Tel-Aviv, Rome, Zurich, and Paris. At our first stop in Athens, I knew we were in for three extraordinary weeks.

Greece is a beautiful country, but it is also a poor country. Everywhere we went, children begged. Although the guides warned us that we should not give them money, it was difficult to ignore them.

"Good American," said the shabby little girl with her hand outstretched.

My heart went out to her, and I reached into my pocket for a quarter. I gently hugged her shoulders and slipped the coin into her hand. THAT WAS ONE BIG MISTAKE! Within minutes, dozens of children surrounded us.

"I warned you," said Brother Taylor. "They are lurking in the shadows, waiting to see how you will respond to their bait. When we get to Cairo, you will find children maimed by their own parents so they can beg for money."

I was not sorry I gave the child the coin, but I did learn that tourists must be aware of the schemes devised to prey upon American hospitality; that it is impossible to be charitable and not create turmoil. We delayed our schedule while the Greek tour guide dispersed the children.

While we were in Athens, there was to be a three-day cruise on the Aegean Sea. The tour agency cancelled it because of turbulent seas and cold weather. To compensate for this, they provided us with a gorgeous excursion to Corinth. Can you imagine the joy it was for me to walk through those ruins where the Apostle Paul once walked and preached? Everything about the place was historically ancient, and yet all around us, I sensed the happenings of the New Testament. They come alive when you can see with your own eyes those places mentioned by Paul in his writings. I must also add that God did not forget Greece when He created the earth. When His first missionaries went forth with the gospel to the Corinthians, they found that He had prepared for them a matchless wonder. The scenic drive from Athens to Corinth is breathtakingly beautiful.

During those three or four days in Greece, we saw many sights and heard much history, not only biblical history, but also ancient world history. One of my highlights of our stay there was the acropolis in Athens. When we climbed that marble-covered mount, the day was drab and rainy; it did not alter our excitement. Words cannot explain the feeling I had when I stood on Mars Hill and looked down upon the ruins of that market place in Athens. It was as though I could hear the Apostle Paul as he cried out to those lost souls who did not know about Jesus. With my Bible open to Acts, chapter 17, those infamous words came to life '...*Ye men of Athens, I perceive that in all things ye are too superstitious. For as I passed by and beheld your devotions, I found an altar with this inscription TO THE UNKNOWN GOD. Whom therefore ye ignorantly worship, him I declare unto you...*'

The following day we boarded a United Arab jet for Cairo. On this flight, I learned about some of the scary and bizarre moments in air travel. The aircraft was about halfway across the Mediterranean when we felt the turbulence. Suddenly, the craft began to rock back and forth, and without a doubt, the flight attendants were rocking too. I soon found one of them sitting in my lap, that is, a flight attendant, and a tray of food! The girl was embarrassed to find herself in such a predicament, but as I told someone later, "All I saw was how pretty she was."

When we finally landed safely in Cairo, airport officials told us to bypass customs and go immediately to the Nile Hilton Hotel. There, we learned that one of the worst sandstorms ever was about to blow in from the Sahara Desert. This was my initial welcoming to Egypt. Little did I know on that day the number of future flights I would be taking in and out of the city of Cairo.

We saw nothing but sand during this entire stay in Egypt. Even while riding the backs of camels, we felt the sting of blowing sand. Nevertheless, the pyramids, the Nile, the ancient mummy museums, and the food only added to this strange and unusual tour.

Before I left Roanoke to go on the tour, Victor Glen, Director of Evangelical Faith Missions, contacted an American missionary in Cairo and told him to look me up at the Nile Hilton Hotel.

"Brother Painter?"

I knew that voice must Guy Troyer, the missionary who had phoned me earlier in the day.

"Yes, and you must be Guy Troyer."

Brother Troyer works with Christian churches in the Cairo area, and I, being a missionary at heart, was more than happy to meet him. We exchanged greetings, and then took a seat in the lobby of the Hilton.

"I have scheduled you to speak for us," Troyer said.

"Me? Oh no, Brother Troyer, I cannot do that. These people could never understand a word I say."

"I have taken care of that. You'll have an interpreter, and a very good one, too."

"Will you come? If you will, I'll pick you up here, and drive you to the church."

I was so amazed at the opportunity that I hardly knew how to respond. Finally, I told him I would go, never realizing how that one single visit would literally change my life forever.

Brother Troyer picked me up that same evening at the Hilton, and while driving across the city, he told me what to expect at the meeting.

Never could he have prepared me for what I found when we arrived at that church. The people were meeting under a crude shelter they used for worship. *(It reminded me of those first days back home in Riverdale).* They came to the meeting in droves, and the longing within their hearts for truth was unbelievable. I spoke on the First Passover and its relationship to the saving blood of Jesus Christ. The response, undoubtedly, was the most extraordinary, beautiful experience I had ever had. My heart was so touched I knew I would never be the same. That night, many Egyptians accepted the Lord Jesus Christ as their personal Savior. I was tee-totally amazed!

Before I left Cairo, God gave me the opportunity to preach at two more meetings, and each time the people's response to the gospel overwhelmed me. He used those three magnificent meetings to place a heavy burden on my heart for those poor, lost, hungry souls.

When the tour group departed from Cairo, I was longing to stay. Thousands of Egyptians were anxious to hear the gospel that was growing old to far too many Americans. I prayed that somehow I could return and reach out to as many of them as possible.

The remaining days of the Holy Land tour were far beyond my expectations. Here we were-visiting all of those places I heard about for so many years. I will never forget the boat rides on the Nile and the Sea of Galilee-walking down the street called Straights-Easter Sunday at Calvary and the Garden Tomb-the Wailing Wall-the Dome of the Rock- Bethlehem-Nazareth, or Bethany. To pray from Mars Hill while overlooking the city of Athens, to walk beneath the olive trees of Gethsemane, and to taste the salty stones fresh from the waters of the Dead Sea are experiences to treasure. This list could go on and on, for as you well know, one can visit many sights in twenty-one days.

Especially will I never forget Easter Sunday morning at Gordon's Calvary and the garden tomb! When we awoke that morning, snow was falling, but soon after breakfast, it turned into rain. Our schedule for Easter was to tour Bethlehem and then return to Jerusalem for a worship service at Gordon's Calvary and the nearby garden tomb. The sun was partially shining when we made the Bethlehem tour, but by the time we were back in Jerusalem, it was cold and raining. Because of the inclement weather, our entire group agreed to remain at the hotel for our

Easter worship service. Hotel management was happy to accommodate us with a large private room on the top floor of the building.

That Easter service in the hotel was in itself quite an experience. Since it was an unplanned event, Brother Art decided we would make it a service of praise. Each member of our tour group had an opportunity to say what the tour had meant to him or her. The meeting progressed, as one would expect it to until three black members took to the floor. You probably can guess what happened. Immediately, the meeting came to life! Two of the black men were ministers who, I must say, did not always behave as such. One of the black deacons, however, was the one who genuinely praised the Lord. He spoke for several minutes, and then said, "I think Williams had better go and sit down." Then, he recalled another place we had visited and his testifying began anew. This probably happened three or four times before "Williams" finally went back to his seat. We were elated. Williams told all that needed to be told, and our hearts were blessed; in addition to that, he entertained us in an amusing way. *(Wherever there was water, Brother Williams was ecstatic. When we visited the Nile, the Jordan, and the Sea of Galilee, he had to have a sample of "holy" water).* When all of the tour members had said what they wished to say at the Easter service, we closed the delightful meeting, grabbed our umbrellas and left for Mount Calvary.

When our group arrived at the traditional site known as Gordon's Calvary, another group of Americans was holding an Easter service. As we huddled together to listen to the singing, all of a sudden, as if it had been staged for a drama, black clouds rolled across the sky, lightning

Jerusalem's Dome of the Rock

flashed, and a clap of thunder roared over the hill. The snow and rain mixture we had previously experienced returned, and up went the umbrellas. What more would a child of God want to see as you stand at the foot of the hill where the Savior died for your sins? God gave to us a moment's re-enactment of that day when His Son hung on the cross. Did I not tell you earlier that this was a most unusual trip?

Finally, we were to leave old Jerusalem and go to the other side of the city. In April of 1967, Jerusalem was a divided city. Leaving the Arabic culture where we had been for almost two weeks, we walked through "no-man's land" into modern day Israel. The guns we saw on either side of us were land markers for both Arab and Jew, and having those weapons pointing at you from two directions was another unnerving experience.

When we arrived on the other side of the city, the Israelis were celebrating Jewish Passover. Throughout the city, there was a flurry of activity. We found our way to the hotel where we enjoyed an elaborate dinner followed by music and folk dancing. The entire program centered on Moses and the Hebrews' exodus out of Egypt. It is too bad they do not understand the spiritual meaning of the Passover.

The following day, after saying good-bye to Jerusalem, we visited an Israeli kibbutz where our Jewish guide gave us a briefing on this communal way of life. The restaurant there, then served us lunch. During the afternoon, we toured an orange grove, crossed the Sea of Galilee by boat, and then enjoyed a delicious St. Peter's fish served by the seaside. After spending a single night in Tiberius, we then motored to Tel Aviv, via Nazareth. We arrived in the coastal city just before sundown and the beginning of the Jewish Sabbath. All was peaceful and quiet.

Following our tour of the Holy Land, our group then visited Rome, Switzerland, and Paris. In Rome, we saw the Coliseum, visited Vatican City, the catacombs, and the Fountain of the Three Coins fame. Several of us, after searching for some time, found the cathedral that houses Michelangelo's statue of Moses. That was a formidable discovery for those of us who had wandered through the streets in search of it.

In Switzerland, we marveled at the magnificent Alps and the people's remarkable lifestyle. After seeing and learning so much old world history for the past two plus weeks, this country's lifestyle was refreshing. Along with the relaxation came the best food we had eaten anywhere, and I could never say enough about the high-posted featherbeds in our Zurich hotel.

Paris was our final stop before coming home. The Louvre, Montmartre, the Eiffel Tower, Mona Lisa; all were remarkable sights.

(On Montmartre, Betty even had her portrait painted with chalk by a French artist)

I would need to write a book to tell about all of the historical places we visited in the spring of 1967, but whoever thought I would ride a camel onto the Sahara Desert, take pictures of skiers on the slopes of the Swiss Alps, or walk through the Roman catacombs where so many Christians lived and died. Today, it would cost a fortune to see and do what we enjoyed in 1967 for less than twelve hundred dollars. Indeed, the entire trip was the opportunity of a lifetime, and it was such a blessing to share it with newfound brothers and sisters in Christ.

Chapter 10

Faithful is He that Calleth

1967-1990

. . . .

"Faithful is he that calleth you, who also will do it."

The Chief of Halawisch Village as seen here with Pastor Saied, Sammy and me

The opportunity afforded me to tour the Middle East in 1967 was a tremendous blessing. To be able to preach to hundreds of Egyptians was something I never dreamed I would do. I have always been overwhelmed that God could use me at all in His service, but to be able to carry the gospel of Jesus Christ halfway around the world was something only a Billy Graham could do. Back at home, I was able to pick up the House of Prayer ministries with even more passion than in the past. At least, this was my way of thinking until an unexpected telephone call in 1975 changed it. "This is Victor Glen, Bob," the voice said from the other end of the line. I need a favor from you." *(Victor Glen is the director of Evangelical Faith Missions, a mission board that the House of Prayer supports.)* "I had a request from Ibrahim Saied," Glen continued, "He is the Egyptian coordinator for Christian missionaries in Cairo, and he needs someone to fill in for

Brother Troyer while he visits the Sudan. Saied wants to know if you will come and do this."

"I don't know," I replied. "I wasn't expecting anything like this. You know how much I love those people over there, but financially, I don't think I could make it happen."

"I understand, but that will not be a problem. The board will take care of the finances."

"Brother Glen, I am completely dumbfounded by your request. How can I refuse?"

"You can't." he chuckled.

"Well, when do you need to know for sure?"

"Take your time. Pray about it, and let me know as soon as you can."

I did pray about the matter, but even before I hung up that telephone receiver, I knew I wanted to go back to Cairo. God had used me there in 1967, and He knew how much I wanted to go there again.

Following my final decision, Satan tried to discourage me in many ways. Every night, I dreamed of airplane crashes, planes on fire, or some other flying accident. I was confident the devil was mad, so I did not waiver in my decision. I was going back to Cairo. So then did Egypt become my *"uttermost part of the earth"*.

Most of Egypt's people live in the narrow fertile valley of the Nile River that flows from South to North and is the world's longest river. They have been there for about 7000 years. Not much is known about its prehistoric history, but we do know that from about 3000 B.C. until 700 B.C., the country had three Kingdoms ruled by strong monarchs. The country prospered during this time, but as each monarch fell, there was stagnation in prosperity. During the Old, Middle, and New Kingdoms substantial construction took place. Many artists and craftmen contributed to their way of life.

Leaders, known as Pharaohs actually began to rule in the first millennium B.C. The ruler was considered to be half god and half man, and anyone approaching a Pharaoh must do so flat on his belly, smelling the earth, crawling on the ground and invoking the 'perfect' god while exalting his beauty.

About 700 B.C., Egyptian life profoundly accelerated due to the influx of foreign powers. During this late period, Egypt prospered and obtained greatness in the eyes of the world. This was the era of the last native kings. At the end of this period, Alexander the Great invaded the country and had himself formally crowned King of Egypt. Egyptian independence then lay dead for 2000 years.

In 304, Ptolemy I ascended to the Egyptian throne. The Ptolemaic period lasted from then until Ptolemy XV Caesarian *(the love child of Caesar and Cleopatra)* was killed by the order of Octavian in 30 B.C. and Rome conquered the country. Thus, it was under Roman rule when Jesus of Nazareth was born to Mary and Joseph.

Egypt came under Arab control in the 600s A.D. From that time, until 1805 when Mohammed Ali became governor, the country began to modernize. Intellectual life was stimulated, foreign capital started to pour in, and liberalism became the order of the day. Several unsuccessful revolutions broke out, and in 1882, the British took over and had control until 1936. In 1922, while the British were there, Egypt became an independent Kingdom. In 1952, King Farouk, the last of the Mohammed Ali dynasty abdicated, and Egypt became a Republic. In 1954, Gamal Abdel Nassar became president and was still in office when I made my first trip to Egypt. Much has happened since 1967. Today, a dictator and members of the native religious community are in power.

Now, that you have a brief summary of Egyptian history, you can see why masses of people in the country are without God. No favorable society has ever had stability. I have made many trips there since 1975, almost on an annual basis. To attempt to cover all that I have seen and done there for the glory of God would be a book within a book. I have had glorious opportunities to preach to hundreds of thousands of people, and have likewise seen thousands make commitments to the Lord Jesus Christ. Egyptians are people starving for the gospel. In order to attend a Christian service, they will walk for many miles. In 1967, there was no freedom to do this, but today the doors are open just as long as you do not approach people in public. Christians are still badly persecuted, but I must say, many freedoms that are allowed by the government came to me as a surprise. For example, Friday is the country's formal day of worship, so most non-Christians do not work on that day. If Christians, however, desire to have Sundays free to worship, then they may do so, but without pay. Many believers lose a day's pay in order to worship

God on Sunday. I wonder how many American Christians would do the same.

My Lab's Final Litter

By the time, I returned from my second missionary trip, I knew it would not be my last. I did not know how I would fund such a mission, but my desire was to preach the gospel in Cairo. Now, most Christians know that when we pray, God will show us a way to make things happen, or He will just simply say no to the requests. Well, sometimes we can as some say, *"put wings on our prayers"*. I suppose that is what I did. Living on top of a mountain, I came up with an idea that would not only benefit my missions' trip, but while I was making the money, I could go about my life as usual. I would breed my chocolate Labrador retriever, and then I would sell her pups. Loving animals the way I do, breeding my dog would be no problem at all, and I could raise the money I needed for my trips. I have continued to go back to Egypt, year after year and I have had a lot of support from my church family and friends, but my puppy sales also helped tremendously.

I cannot begin to tell you all that has happened to the Christian Egyptian community since 1967. The people I first preached to, *(those worshipping under the shelter on the street)* now have a five-story church that covers a city block in Cairo. The building has three large auditoriums. I have seen all three packed so tightly that not another person could get in. At the time of my first return trip, there were only two Christian churches anywhere in the city. Today, if I were to book a three-week stay and preach somewhere different every night, I could not begin to accommodate the churches requesting meetings. I have preached in 28 villages from Upper Egypt to Cairo, and all of these villages are increasing in their number of Christian churches. I have seen everything, from a sizeable live turkey standing right in front of me while I ate to being in a home where a water buffalo gave birth to a calf. God always took care of us. For sixteen years, not Bob, John, Ed, Jeffery, Steve, Guy, Doris, or I were ever sick.

Satan fights back. Every time Christians build a church in Cairo, another religion purchases land and erects a building next to it. Many Christians are persecuted for witnessing to others; however, Christian missionaries are relatively safe. The Egyptian Secret Services and local police protect those of us who go for revivals. It is not against the law to witness to an Egyptian who comes to you, but you cannot approach someone who does not. That is why all Christian activities must be coordinated.

Egyptians are converting to Christianity by the thousands. For most of them, their conversions are genuine because too much is at stake for pretense. On my first return trip to Cairo, three men came to meet me with a donkey. They were Said's brother-in-law, an owner of a fleet of taxis, and a rock-n-roll singer. All three men were saved while I was there. They immediately began growing strong in the Lord, and today they all are pastors of large Christian churches and are winning hundreds of souls to the Lord. Suppose I had not gone when Brother Glen called. Those men may have never found Jesus as their Savior.

Here in America, we do not encounter satanic forces that are so prevalent in non-Christian nations. This makes it easy for Christians here to underestimate demonic powers. In Egypt, I witnessed it first-hand. I saw a young demon-possessed woman weighing less than ninety pounds take on two husky men and toss them around like a rubber ball. I have heard voices coming from human beings that were everything but human, and I have seen the power of God bring these forces under control. Someone once said that with the decline of Christianity in America, we are apt to see some of these demonic forces at work here. I believe this could happen.

I learned much from my time with the Egyptian missionaries and Christian interpreters. God will use anyone who is willing to be broken for His use. One of my interpreters, Dr. Wadia, is a neurosurgeon in Cairo. I am sure he daily puts his job at risk by serving Jesus Christ. On one occasion, he would not allow me to leave without a gift of 200 pounds. I gave it to two missionaries working there with children. Doris Gross, a missionary of the House of Prayer, was working there, and we learned through her that the second missionary was a German girl named Dora. They used the money to buy art supplies for the children.

I am thankful also for fellow believers who have helped me in this foreign ministry. A number of friends have traveled with me to the other side of the world. Brothers Bob Miller, Ed Robtison, John Ingram, Steve Manley, and Jeffery Wayne Clarke have at one time or another, been with me. I believe God uses friends to assist us in our ministries, and I graciously thank every one of them. Others, who could not go with me, have given financial support. Indeed am I grateful to all who have kept me in their prayers. As someone has said, *"It remains to be seen what God can accomplish when His people pray."*

Egypt is not the only foreign missions the House of Prayer supports. Contributions to Oriental Missionary Society, Evangelical Faith Ministries, G.T. Bustin, Indian Missions, Christ's Ambassadors, the Davis family's Mexican orphanage and clinic, and the Blue Ridge Holiness Camp are ongoing. The church also contributes to Miriam Peters, a missionary sent by the Floyd House of Prayer.

Unseen Harvest

Much can be gained from a seed in the hand
Sown by a tiller who loves the land
He'll feed and water each growing vine
Plucking the fruit at just the right time
Take, Lord, my offering-this seed from my hand
Place with another in some distant land
Sow in abundance the truth from your word
Nurturing men who never have heard
A Savior died, their souls to redeem
May they be the fruit of my tiny seed

John Ingram and Bob Miller

Solomon, Wayne Clark, and Samir

**An American Graduation with
Irene Saied, Ginny, and me**

**Cairo Greeting with Doris Gross, Ed
Robtison, Bob Miller, the Saieds and me**

Chapter 11

Finishing the Work

1971-1990

. . . .

"I have finished the work which thou gavest me to do."

During the seventies and eighties, all of the ministries at the House of Prayer continued to reach out to the community, and until the year of 1982, I continued with the ministries of the congregation in Floyd County. In addition to these two church ministries, I returned almost annually to Egypt for a series of meetings there.

Here at home, things were happening in people's lives where they needed prayer and help from their minister. On August 15, 1974, a real tragedy took place in our midst, a tragedy no one understood. Jimmy Holley was a young man who loved the Lord. He found salvation in June of 1974, and went forward in a July camp meeting to commit his life for service to God. Jimmy planned to attend a Bible college after his graduation, but on August 15, at a House of Prayer picnic, the beloved lad drowned in Smith Mountain Lake. His home going was a hard pill to swallow, especially for his parents who had just seven years earlier lost their little girl, Peggy. Their grief was heartbreaking for the House Prayer's entire congregation. In honor of Jimmy, every fifth Sunday of a month at the church, our offerings go to a college fund that helps young people with a Christian education.

There are times when we clearly see God is at work, and there are times when I feel as though He just simply tells us no. Baby Suzette Leigh Leonard was certainly NOT one of those times that God was saying no. If ever we saw one, she was a miracle child. Suzette was born on December 29, 1977 with a birth defect, Spinal Bifida. The doctors told Hillary and Betty, Suzette's parents, that there was little hope that she would live. If she did survive, more than likely, she would have mental retardation, and furthermore, she probably would never be able to walk. Four days after she was born, the baby had surgery to close her opened spine. Eight days later, fluid started gathering on her head, and doctors performed a second surgery to insert a shunt.

Brother Clayton Leonard, Hillary's brother, was a minister of the gospel, Together, we went to pray for little Suzette. As we were driving to the hospital, I told Clayton I was confident that the baby was going to be all right. That was, however, very difficult for anyone to believe. Even though many Christians prayed for little Suzette, her healing appeared to be hopeless.

Suzette survived that bout with her affliction and went home with her parents. When she was two years old, she was back in the hospital with a kidney infection. Physicians told the parents that the cut-off valves from the kidneys to the bladder were not working. To correct the problem, they would have to operate and insert artificial valves. Again, members of the House of Prayer went to their knees, and once more, her mother and father took her home. Friends and family continued to pray for Suzette and to thank God for all that He had done on her behalf. One year later, she had a physical check-up.

"I cannot believe what I am seeing on these x-rays," the physician said. "Everything appears to be normal."

"Doctor," Betty addressed the man, "Hillary and I are Christians so we committed our baby to the Lord. We have prayed, our friends have prayed, and apparently, God has healed her."

When mother and child left his office, Suzette's doctor was in tears.

Suzette grew into a sweet Christian girl, graduating from Roanoke Valley Christian Schools. She then moved to Florida where she graduated from Palm Beach Atlantic College with a degree in Marketing. Her sister, Ginger lives in Florida, so Suzette stayed there. Today, she has a healthy son and daughter and works as a lawyer's assistant.

For many years, members of the Leonard family were supporters of our work at the House of Prayer. They came to us from cottage prayer meetings, revivals, and tent meetings in Botetourt County. These people truly love the Lord, and several are in full-time Christian service.

Right here, I will tell you the story about the healing of Brother Cecil Wimmer. As I said previously, this man was a faithful servant of God and dedicated to the House of Prayer ministries. Because of Charlotte's marriage to Cecil, Jr. (Buddy), Brother Cecil was also a dear friend.

I have always believed God hears the prayers of His people and answers them according to His will. Sometimes, we do not know what that will is, so He reveals it to us through answered prayer. In October of 1977, Cecil had a massive heart attack. When his doctors talked with the family, they told us that he probably would not make it through the night. Immediately, House of Prayer members prayed. With Cecil's faith and Christians praying, God intervened. Cecil was home before Christmas.

The year that followed was one of many return visits to the hospital, and each time the family would hear there was no hope for Cecil's recovery. Every time I went into that room, I came out believing he was going to be all right.

In October of 1978, a year after his first massive attack, the medical staff at Roanoke Memorial Hospital told the family they had done all that they could do. Cecil's heart was so out of rhythm that it was literally beating itself to death. Because of Duke University Hospital's expertise, his doctors sent him there for treatment. This was an enormous undertaking, and Cecil insisted that his desire was for God's will. Back at the church, people prayed and gave love offerings to help offset his expenses.

Cecil once again returned home, and he was an active man for at least 6 years. His heart finally played out in June of 1984. He travelled to Richmond for the funeral of a nephew killed in an automobile accident. On Monday morning following his return home, Viola found him asleep in the arms of Jesus. He had peaceably gone to heaven in his sleep.

Before I finish telling you the story of my life, I must tell you about an unusual working of God in another couple's life. Joyce worked in the office for the Kroger Company, and she had a young supervisor there by the name of Charles Minucie. He loved to hunt so one day Joyce invited him to come and hunt with me. "I know Daddy would love for you to come up," Joyce said. "He loves having someone to hunt with him."

When hunting season arrived, we had a new hunter-Charles. Immediately, I took to the young man, and I think he liked me too. For the next 14 or 15 years, he was our guest during hunting season. Sometimes Charles would even come and cut firewood for me. Whenever I talked with him about the Lord, I sensed he was not interested. He and his wife, Debbie went to church, and Charles had professed Christ as a youth at Tabernacle Baptist Church in Salem. I just suppose he never grew in the Lord, so my observations led me to believe that he was still a lost soul. Regardless of where they stood spiritually, I prayed for Charles and his wife for a number of years. One day, just before I was to leave on one of my trips to Egypt, he and Debbie came to bring me a box of goodies she had baked for the trip. "Pray for me while I'm gone," I said

Immediately Debbie replied, "I will do that."

Debbie did try to pray for me, but in doing so, the Holy Spirit started to deal with her heart, and she realized she was lost. Becoming much convicted of sin in her life, she confessed that she was a sinner and gave her heart to the Lord.

Charles, on the other hand, did not believe his wife when she told him of her salvation, but as time passed, he knew something had happened to her because she was a different person than the one he had known before. One night I was conducting a Bible Study in Rocky Mount, and I invited Charles and Debbie. That night God spoke to Charles' heart and on the way home from the meeting, He continued to deal with him. Charles needed assurance of his salvation, and he asked God to give it to him. In a very odd way, God answered. Charles was collecting comic books for his children, and for some reason, he could not stop thinking about those comic books. It was as if they might be coming between him and the Lord. Charles decided to get rid of them. After he did this, he regained the assurance of his salvation. The next day, his heart was rejoicing in song, especially with *"Go Tell It on the Mountain"*. He

94

wanted somebody to know what had happened, but Debbie was out shopping, and Charles could not reach Bob Miller or me. Finally, he decided to go up on the mountain for target practice. His friend, Randy, showed up, and the next thing Charles knew he was talking to him about the Lord. This, he had never before done. A few weeks later, he shared this experience with a pastor who told him that God must have given him that song to get him up on the mountain to witness. Charles' response was 'We serve a God who is simply amazing!'

Many months passed, and one day Charles had a phone call from... guess who? It was the comic book dealer. He needed a prayer warrior for his wife, and he knew where to find one-the man who brought him back the comic books so he could please the Lord. The comic book incident was no longer a mystery for Charles.

Later, I told Charles that one day he was going to be a preacher, but he did not believe me. The next thing I knew, he was helping me with the radio ministry. Later, he studied Hebrew with an Israeli woman and eventually earned a PhD from Jacksonville Theological Seminary.

Charles and Debbie joined the West Salem Baptist Church where they continued to grow in the Lord. This was truly a glorious and blessed experience!

Now that I have told you about all of the blessings in my life, I suppose I should say something about conflicts. We all face a crisis at one time or another, one that we simply cannot understand. Our human nature leads us to believe we are in control, when actually our Heavenly Father is the one who is at the helm. I have loved every moment I have spent in service for my Lord, but it is still difficult for me to understand when He tells me no. I simply forget that nothing is going to happen to me that He is not permitting. Sometimes, I do not hear Him speak because I am too busy not listening. Aging saints are the most vulnerable to these mistakes. We have done something for so long, we cannot let go. Fifty

House of Prayer Pastors, Brothers Steve Parker, Robert Painter and Jeff Keaton

years or so into the ministry, I found myself in exactly this situation. As a result, my heart was broken.

Everyone who has held the same position, or followed the same line of work for a lifetime finds it difficult to step into retirement, but when our careers are full-time Christian service, we tend to think we are different. This could not be further from the truth. We are all human beings, and we all have the same vulnerabilities. My people know how much I love the House of Prayer. It was my heartbeat for almost half of a century. Leaving the pastorate there was akin to leaving your life behind. Because of this, it was just downright hard for me to let go. I now see the growth of House of Prayer ministries, and I realize that God needed someone there to lead who was young, enthusiastic, and vibrantly strong. I thank Him so much for sending Brothers Steve Parker and Jeff Keaton to carry on the work. Brother Parker led the church into the building of its first new sanctuary, moving the location to Hardy Road in Roanoke County. With the Blue Ridge Parkway nearby, the church changed its name to Parkway House of Prayer. Under the leadership of Brother Keaton, the congregation has more than doubled in number. A Christian school with grades K-12 is blossoming, and the church has actually outgrown the new building. My prayers are with my people that they will remember the purpose and the principles upon which we founded the church, that it will not compromise the fundamentals of the Christian faith and that people will stay unified as a body of believers.

I am now 92 years old. The years have passed swiftly. There have been times of blessings and times of testing. I have rejoiced in the Lord, and I have shed many tears. I have been on the mountaintop, and I have walked through dark valleys. I am still just an unworthy sinner saved by the grace of Almighty God.

Ginny and I are both feeble in mind and body. God has given us 70 years together as man and wife. Our love has only grown sweeter with the years. We know our time on earth is limited, but we are ready to go when God calls. My prayer is that when I depart from this life, I will enter heaven with Jesus as my escort. I want to touch His nail-scarred hands then look into his eyes, and say, "thank you." I then want to be with my family who has gone before me. I want to greet those people who knelt at that altar in Jordantown, and all of those who ever passed through the doors of the House of Prayer and our little church in Floyd. I want to shake the hands of friends, co-workers, neighbors, prisoners, and hospital patients, and when I have met all of them, I want to listen to testimonies from radio listeners, revival converts, and those Egyptians I won to the Savior, but never knew. Finally, I want to see Jesus for the second time. I want to stand there in His presence and say, as did the Apostle Paul to Timothy, "I have fought a good fight, I have finished my course, and I have kept the faith…" Then, I must add, "No, Lord, it wasn't me. It was always you."

The End

Robert and Virginia Morgan Painter

Gloria Painter Beckner, Joyce Painter Hudson, Charlotte Painter Wimmer

Epilogue

. . . .

My interviews with Brother Painter took place a number of years ago, probably ten years before his death. Many things happened in his life during those years. Some of them were pleasant happenings, and some were tragic. There was one event, though, that was exceptionally pleasing to Brother Painter. His daughter, Charlotte, decided that she too, would go in search of her *"uttermost part of the earth"*.

Charlotte Painter Wimmer

In 2004, after a heart-warming Bible study, Charlotte began searching as to what more she could be doing for the Lord. This led her to pray that God's will would be done in her life. She told the Lord if He opened a door of service for her, she would endeavor to walk through that door. Shortly thereafter, she heard of a request from the Southern Baptist Mission Board. They needed volunteers to cook for all of their Asian missionaries soon to be on a retreat in Malaysia. The mission board was expecting one hundred people to attend. Charlotte had only flown once, and she had cried throughout the flight. Nevertheless, she volunteered for this missionary assignment.

At this time in the Painter family, much prayer was in the offering. Its members were experiencing both tragedy and heartbreak. Ginny was bedfast with Alzheimer's disease, Brother Painter was confined to a wheelchair as a result of strokes, and Gloria's breast cancer, in remission for fourteen years, had returned and metastasized in the spine. Any one of these family members was subject to leave for heaven while Charlotte was away. Nevertheless, the family was of one accord, Charlotte should keep her commitment to God.

Thinking that she was going to be part of a large team of workers, Charlotte began to relax. It was not long before she learned that a young girl, just recently married, was the only other volunteer. Of course, this meant that because of her age and experience in cooking, Charlotte would be in charge of planning the menus. She would also prepare a list of groceries the cooks would need. This senior volunteer became panicky. She could not sleep at night for worry.

Gloria, always known to be the planner and organizer, came to her sister's rescue. Together, they planned every meal Charlotte would need to prepare. On her menus, they included what they deemed to be the most well liked foods-Thanksgiving, Christmas, Italian, Southern, and Southwestern. There was even a Mississippi Mud Pie. One request for a specific food came from the missionaries who would attend the retreat-country ham for breakfast. If permitted, the women could bring the ham and the missionaries would pay for it.

Charlotte purchased the ham, had it sliced and sealed in packages. When the two women were packing their bags, they placed the ham in different pieces of their luggage.

Soon, the cooks were on their way to the Far East. All went well until they passed through customs in South Korea. Charlotte's helper had her luggage flagged, and part of their country ham was confiscated. Of course, the young helper was terrified, but the problem was soon resolved. The Koreans do not allow "pig" to come into their country so they would keep the country ham, and the travelers could be on their way. However, the two women must still answer one simple question, "How does one prepare the meat for consumption?" Later, in Malaysia, the missionaries were able to enjoy some of the country ham because those packages hidden in Charlotte's bags were safe.

After finally arriving in Malaysia, our two *"missionaries in training"* found a number of surprises, but none as shocking as their kitchen facilities. There, they found but a little space for preparing food, and their appliances consisted of two propane burners and a single oven. After viewing this, Charlotte was wondering why she had ever volunteered for this project!

The country of Malaysia is located near the equator so the heat there is almost unbearable. One day as Charlotte was at work in the kitchen, Pastor Jim Austin walked into the room. "My hair," she tells everyone, "looked as though it had just been shampooed, and I was drenched with perspiration." The pastor became extremely upset that the women had such working conditions, and immediately requested fans for them. Charlotte pointed to the ceiling where several fans were already in operation. All they could do was circulate the hot, humid air.

While the missionaries were enjoying a "little taste of home" with Charlotte's cooking, her family, friends, and church family back at home were praying for her success and wellbeing. When she finally returned safely, they learned that God answered their prayers. He had truly blessed her, her helper, and the missionaries. Most of all, He honored Charlotte's promise that she would go and serve by erasing her fears of flying.

Soon after Charlotte's departure for Malaysia, Gloria's doctor, after seeing her fight for her life, requested Hospice care for her. His patient learned that Hospice could not administer the fluids she needed, so the gravely ill Gloria declined the care. She wanted to wait for her sister to return home and tell her about the missions' trip. Not long after Charlotte was home, Gloria asked her husband, Jim, to call Hospice and again ask for their help. Her family knew then that she was in much pain.

As time passed, the pain was so excruciating, Gloria wanted to go home to heaven. Even after Hospice nurses were unable to get a pulse, she lived on. "Do you suppose," a nurse asked Joyce, "there is some unfinished business?"

Jim and Gloria Painter Beckner

Joyce, at her sister's bedside, replied. "Maybe she wants to hear Daddy's voice one more time. He is not able to come here, but I'll go and ask him to call her."

As Joyce puts it, "That phone call was one of the hardest things I have ever had to do."

After telling her daddy of Gloria's condition, Joyce waited a few moments for his emotions to calm. She then picked up the phone, dialed the number, and handed the phone to her father. "I then left the room," she told me, "because I could not bear to listen."

Moments after her daddy prayed with her, Gloria went to heaven.

With her heart breaking, Joyce retreated to her flower garden. Just as she always does in times of trouble, she began to pull weeds from among her flowers. Her husband, Don, joined her, and the two of them silently worked side by side.

I think I am going to lose it, thought Joyce, as she continued to work, and if I do, what will happen to Mom and Dad. Lord, help me; this was her silent prayer.

"Suddenly," Joyce said as she continued her story, "I felt the very presence of the Holy Spirit." That simple prayer was so much like those that Daddy prayed, and although it was just a prayer within my heart, God heard me. 'Have faith in me'. That was what He told me; not just once, but over and over again."

Joyce dropped the garden hoe she was working with and went into the house. After searching a hymnal for words of comfort, she found these words, 'He understands your grief and your sorrow'. The tears then came, and she knew her God was at her side. He answered her prayer and gave to her the strength she needed to carry her burden.

Gloria had met her husband, Jim Beckner while they were both working for General Electric. He wanted her to marry him, but because of one failed marriage, Gloria had refused. Later, with her diagnosis of cancer, Jim was faithful and proved his love in many ways, asking her again to marry him.

"Why would you even consider marrying someone with cancer?" Gloria had asked.

"Because I love you, and I want to take care of you."

Finally, Gloria consented, and the couple married. The cancer went into remission, and Gloria lived for another 14 years. Jim's two sons became Gloria's and her one son came to love his new father. It was a beautiful and happy marriage-truly a devoted family!

Jim was a terrific caregiver, keeping his promise to care for Gloria. After her death, he gave her family a letter she had written for them while Charlotte was in Malaysia. She shared with them memories from the past, and thanked them all for the encouragement and support they had given her. She then wrote these words of encouragement-Stay strong in the faith.

Joyce, Don, and Charlotte all agree to this one reflection, 'Dad taught us how we should live BY faith, and Gloria taught us how to die IN the faith'. Their sister's favorite verses were Philippians 4:11-13.

Ginny's Alzheimer disease steadily progressed until her death in 2006. The Painter family once again suffered a significant loss. Losing two of the people he most loved in a span of two years, Brother Painter, age 92, exercised his faith more than ever. His greatest consolation was the brevity of time before he would reunite with Gloria and Ginny. His own medical problems were numerous, and he was in need of much care. Joyce and Charlotte agree that God sent them many devoted caregivers. Those who came with much love in their hearts were Andrea, Lee, Debbie, Nancy, Melissa, and Nova. They were there either before or after the death of Ginny. Brother Painter's two girls will never forget the loving care they gave to their father and mother, this great man of God and his dear wife.

After the death of Ginny, Joyce and Don moved into the Painter home and became his caregivers for the next nine months. His house was better equipped for his needs than was their own. Don cared for his father-in-law as if he were his own father. Not once complaining, he was always there to do whatever was necessary. Joyce gives nothing but praise for her husband's devotion to her father. I am confident Brother Painter did the same.

Don and Joyce Painter Hudson

In 2007, Brother Painter fell and broke several toes. Knowing his diabetes would complicate the healing, he was taken to a hospital emergency room. From there, he went to Carrington Place, a Botetourt County nursing facility where he would live out his final days. That was a sad day for Joyce, Charlotte, and their dad. Joyce says that when she left him, she was in tears. She prayed that he would adjust to his new environment and that he would be able to be of service to those around him. His life had been lived to serve others, and that is what he would want to be doing for as long as possible. A few days later, he told a former caregiver, "I am exactly where I need to be, and I like it here very much."

At the nursing home, Brother Painter had a room with a view of the mountains he so dearly loved. He made many new friends, and even had some old friends living there. He attended Bible study and worship services and had tons of visitors. His final days were truly happy ones!

GOD IS GOOD! The last time I saw Brother Painter he was on the porch of Carrington Place chatting with three of my cousins, Uncle Bob and Aunt Florence Mays' girls. Always faithful to his ministry, they had not forgotten the man who gave so much and received so little in return.

No, Robert Painter was not a man of eminent fame-his name not one to be known in every household; however, being the humble man that he was, I believe he preferred it to be that way. If, however, you were to travel up and down the basin of the Nile River, or attend a Christian church meeting in Cairo, I think you would find masses of Christian believers who know his name. They will tell you that when they were but children, he came to their villages, or preached to them on city streets. They would tell you how they ran to him year after year, throwing their little arms around his neck, and that when he left to go home, how they pleaded for him to stay. I think also that hundreds, or even thousands of them might say, 'He told us about Jesus'.

I, too, was but a child when Mama took me to 17th Street for a church service on a Sunday afternoon and I have not forgotten either. All I have written here is but to say, "Thank you, Lord, for allowing me to be a part of this man's ministry. May telling Brother Painter's story bring honor to your Son, our Lord and Savior, Jesus Christ, and to your faithful servant who was loved by all who knew him."

Betty Hutchinson, 1947

Robert L. Painter, *"The Preacher"* went to be with the Lord on April 11, 2008. Surviving him are two daughters, eight grandchildren, and fourteen great-grandchildren. In obedience to the will of God, he was an extraordinary man who lived an extraordinary life.

Here is but a sample of the legacy he left behind:

Minsters/Theologians:

Dr. Charles Minucie, PhD
Dr. Debbie Minucie, PhD
Dr. Donald M. Hudson, PhD
Rev. Rick Barton
Rev. Jack Beckner
Rev. Benjamin Fulton
Rev. Richard Hall
Rev. John Ingram
Rev. Clayton Leonard
Rev. Robert Miller
Rev. Kenneth Wright
Numerous Egyptian Pastors

Missionaries:

Rev. Harold Cadd

Ms. Miriam Peters Gregory
Ms. Doris Gross

(There are scores of deacons, Sunday school teachers, musicians, and other Christian workers in the U.S. and Egypt)

Testimonials:

We called him The Preacher! He wanted to be a farmer, an outdoorsman (hunting, fishing, etc.), but he was called to be a preacher. Nobody called him Robert, that is, no one but Sister Painter when she was being stern. He was The Preacher!

When I met him, he was probably 79 years old. At age 80, he took my son, Sean (age 16) and Donnie Carter (18) to make hay. He worked them so hard that they did not go back the next day. I told Sean if The Preacher had been 79, he would have worked them to death.

Loading llama manure, climbing a cherry tree at age 80, taking a shopping trip on a Saturday, or one across the ocean...coming or going, there was a Bible lesson straight from his memory. If there was a question you needed to have answered, you could use him as a Bible commentary or concordance.

He was 87 years old when he made his final trip to Egypt, and almost blind, he preached from memory. When he began to preach, the years melted away. Once he started to preach, he looked twenty years younger.

As he traveled to outlying villages of the Nile, he gave directions to the Egyptian cab drivers who didn't know where they were to turn. The Preacher remembered for he had been there before-perhaps a year or two before.

The Preacher gave directions wherever he was-the direction to heaven. Would not it be interesting to know how many people he introduced to Jesus? How many of his converts were in full-time Christian service? How many souls are in heaven because he was a faithful servant?

Today, II Timothy 4:2 comes to mind; "Preach the word; be instant in season, out of season; reprove, rebuke, exhort with all longsuffering and doctrine." You didn't ask The Preacher to preach unless you were ready because he was ready in season, out of season, all seasons.

I was privileged to drive him here and there in the evening years of his life. I witnessed many events that you knew God had to do!

I miss him very much! How often do you get to spend so much time with a man God chose to make great? Because he answered the call, many stories could be told about the times he prayed over the sick, babies, etc., but the first three words of II Timothy 4:2 covers them all, "PREACH THE WORD". This is what Robert Painter did, so we just called him The Preacher.

Bob Miller (Rev. Robert Miller)

Thanks for telling the next generation the story of Rev. Robert L. Painter. His whole life was truly a miracle of God's grace and a revelation of what the Lord will do when a life is yielded to Him.

I grew up as a preacher's kid, one whose father, Rev. Dan Parker, had a friend we all knew as "Preacher Painter." My dad told me stories so often about this preacher that he became a living legend in my mind. During the 1960s, Brother Painter pastored two churches in the Roanoke Valley of Virginia, and Dad, along with several other friends, held many revival meetings in both churches called The House of Prayer. Dad always came home from these meetings overjoyed, telling us how God moved mightily in the services-that the altars were lined with people seeking God. (Little did I know then that many of those souls who gave their hearts to God during those revivals I would one day pastor).

Dad also shared with his kids many stories "The Preacher" told about life in the Blue Ridge Mountains. Many times the stories were true, but sometimes they were tales that were almost unbelievable, and yet all of us listening to them were spellbound.

As a teenager, I began singing with a group known as the "Young Witnesses". One night, during a revival service, we were singing in Wyo, North Carolina. It was there, I finally met the man called Robert Painter. Like everyone who knew him, I immediately liked him, and I deeply admired his ministry. Later, just as my father before me, I had the privilege to conduct revival services for him in both of his churches. Because of my father's admiration for him, I felt a connection to this great man of God, and I loved the people he was pastoring. It was after our revival at the Roanoke House of Prayer that Brother Painter retired, and I was contacted to replace him. God made it clear to me that I was to go and try my best to fill those great big shoes. I never dreamed that I would find such wonderful people, the sheep of Robert Painter's flock.

When finally I had settled into the House of Prayer pastorate, I came to know the reality of those legends buried deep within my heart and the reality of the awesome responsibility given me to continue the legacy "The Preacher" had begun. His accomplishments still amaze me.

I am blessed to have known R.L. Painter, and I am thankful that for half of a century, he remained faithful to the task before him. His memory lives on in his people, and the results of his efforts will live on throughout eternity.

Glad to be serving Jesus,
Pastor Stephen A. Parker, Parkway House of Prayer

When we think about the people who have had the greatest influence on our lives, we find Brother Robert Painter to be at the top of the list. He was like a parent to the young people of the House of Prayer, always reminding us to find God's will for our lives. His own personal testimony of salvation, his love for people, his faith, and his calling from the Lord to be a minister of the gospel affected the lives of all who knew him as a pastor and friend.

In addition to working a full-time job to support his family, Brother Painter pastored our church, planned church events, revival meetings, and tent revivals-some in remote locations. Brother Painter was a man of convictions and lived them even when others disagreed with him. "The Preacher" was undoubtedly a living testimony to all who knew him. It was an honor to have served under his leadership at The House of Prayer in Roanoke, Virginia during the early years of his ministry. It is also a blessing, even today, to have known his friendship.

Roger G. and Mildred H. St. Clair
Covington, Georgia
House of Prayer Pianist 1948-1954

- Brother Painter was a man of prayer, and he was always faithful to the end.
- He knew his Bible better than anyone I ever met.
- He always loved to share vegetables from his garden with friends and neighbors.
- He thoroughly enjoyed hunting and fishing.
- Brother Painter was never too old to sleigh ride and throw snowballs.
- Many souls were saved under the ministry of Brother Painter.
- People just do not forget a man like him. He will live on for he was a blessing to many.
- Brother Painter was faithful; rain or snow, he was there. They did not stop him.
- If God truly calls men to serve him then I believe Brother Painter was such a man.

(Anniversary Testimonials from Roanoke and Floyd House of Prayer Family)

Afterword

R obert Painter was an ardent supporter of Sam and Nancy Davis, missionaries to Mexico. In 2010, as the couple was traveling down a highway 70 miles south of the border town of Reynosa, Mexico, drug thugs shot and fatally wounded Nancy with a bullet to her head. The Christian missionaries were well aware of the escalating drug violence in Mexico and gunmen had chased them on previous occasions. Nancy earlier told a friend, "We know when we go back in, we might not come back alive, and if that's the case, know that we died doing what we were supposed to do. If I don't see you again here, I'll see you in heaven."

Nancy was probably welcomed home by another saint who also loved the souls of men, Brother Robert Painter.

The Greeting

When I behold my Savior's face
On golden streets by crystal sea
I will hold His hands in mine
Touch those nail prints made by me

Let me press the side I wounded
Where my sin His life's blood bore
To satisfy the wrath of God
This righteous flesh of life I tore

Dare I kiss two feet that spilt
Holy blood on Calvary's Mount
It paid a debt no man could pay
And covers sins no man can count

Oh, to brush those lips of Truth
Caress the brow I crowned with thorns
Then whisper 'thank you' one more time
And say 'I love you' to my Lord

Printed in the United States
By Bookmasters